Being Jesus'
Disciple

PUBLISHING

Torrance, California

© 2010 Bristol Works, Inc.
Rose Publishing, Inc.
4733 Torrance Blvd., #259
Torrance, California 90503 U.S.A.
Email: info@rose-publishing.com
www.rose-publishing.com

Free, downloadable study guide at rose-publishing.com. Click on "News & Info," then on "Downloads."

Includes these Rose Publishing Titles:

Who I am in Christ ©2010 Bristol Works, Inc.
   Authors: William Brent Ashby, BT; Benjamin Galan, MTS, ThM
Knowing God's Will ©2006, 2009 RW Research, Inc.
Spiritual Disciplines ©2009 Bristol Works, Inc.
   Authors: William Brent Ashby, BT; Benjamin Galan, MTS, ThM
Why Truth Matters: 10 Common Doctrinal Errors ©2010 Bristol Works, Inc.
   Author: Robert M. Bowman, Jr., MA
What the Bible Says about Money ©2009 Bristol Works, Inc.
   Author: Jessica Curiel, MA
24 Ways to Explain the Gospel ©2009 Bristol Works, Inc.
   Authors: William Brent Ashby, BT; Benjamin Galan, MTS, ThM
Strong in the Storm: 6 Lessons from Persecuted Christians ©2010 Bristol Works, Inc.
   Contributors: Writers and researchers of Open Doors USA and Open Doors International

Many of these titles are available as individual pamphlets, as wall charts, and as ready-to-use PowerPoint® presentations.

Library of Congress Cataloging-in-Publication Data

Being Jesus' disciple.
   p. cm. – (Rose Bible basics)
ISBN 978-1-59636-415-8 (pbk.)
1. Christian life. 2. Christian life–Biblical teaching. I. Rose Publishing (Torrance, Calif.)
BV4501.3.B436 2011
248.4–dc22
                        2010033826

Printed by Regent Publishing Services Ltd.
Printed in China
November 2010, First printing

Being Jesus' Disciple

Contents

Continued
on next
page

Being Jesus' Disciple

Contents

Who I am in Christ

Your True Identity

Assurance of Salvation

Being Made in the Image of God

The Meaning of "Christian"

who i am

because of what he has done

Because Jesus died, he can offer forgiveness. Because Jesus rose from the dead, he can give us life and victory. Forgiveness, life, and victory give us identity. We now live forgiven, abundant and victorious lives. Our lives are not perfect since we still experience pain and suffering. However, our hope is firm because it is based on Jesus' victory over death.

I am forgiven.

Eph. 1:6–8; Rom. 8:1, 38

All my sins are forgiven before God. God will not condemn me for:

- Bad things I have done.
- Good things I have left undone.
- Evil things I have said.
- Wrong things I have thought.

I am reconciled with God.

Rom. 5:10; 2 Cor. 5:18–19; Col. 1:21–22; Heb. 10:19–22

- I have been reunited with God.
- The anger that was between us is gone.
- Because of Jesus, I now have free access to God.

I am rescued.

Matt. 20:28; 1 Tim. 2:5–6

- I have been rescued from a life-threatening situation.
- Jesus paid the ransom for my life with his own life.
- Sin no longer holds my life hostage.

I am redeemed.

Eph. 1:13–14; Col. 1:14; Titus 2:14; Heb. 9:12; 1 Peter 1:18

- I have had my life debt covered, and my future holds an inheritance from God.
- My life is no longer a worthless debt to sin.
- I now look forward to rich meaning and purpose in God's future plan for me.

I am bought with a price and belong to God.

1 Cor. 6:19–20; 7:23

- I have been paid for by God.
- God owns me.
- I no longer belong to myself.
- My old way of life no longer owns me.

I am known by God.

Rom. 8:29; 2 Tim. 2:19

- I have been known and cared about all along.
- God has been watching out for me from the beginning.
- God has cared for me from day one.

in CHRiST

I am chosen.

Rom. 8:30; Eph. 1:4; 1 Peter 2:9

- *I have been hand picked by God.*
- *My salvation was not accidental. God intended it for me.*
- *God called me out for salvation, even though I do not deserve it.*

I am justified before God.

Rom. 3:23–26, 5:1, 8:1, 30

- *God has declared me innocent because of Christ.*
- *Jesus has won my case by paying my penalty for me.*
- *I have been acquitted of all my crimes.*

I am accepted.

Rom. 15:7; Eph. 1:4-6; 1 Peter 2:10

- *I have been welcomed by God.*
- *I am no longer rejected.*
- *I am no longer an outsider.*

I am saved.

Rom. 5:8–10; 7:13–25; Eph. 2:1–10; Col. 1:13

I have been rescued:

- *From God's just anger.*
- *From sin.*
- *From myself.*
- *From death.*
- *From Satan and a sinful system.*

I am alive.

Rom. 6:11; 8:9–11; Eph. 2:4–5

- *I have received new life from God.*
- *My spirit has been brought to life and will never be dead again.*
- *My body will be made new after I die and I will live forever.*
- *I have new meaning and purpose and a new way of looking at life.*

I am free.

John 8:32-36; Rom. 6:22–23; Gal. 4:7; 5:1

- *I have been set free.*
- *I am no longer a slave to sin.*

I am secure.

Rom. 8:28, 31–38

- *I know that God works things for my good in all circumstances.*
- *I am free from all condemnation.*
- *I know that nothing can separate me from the love of God.*

I am sealed.

2 Cor. 1:21–22

I am safe because God has:

- *Anointed me.*
- *Set his seal of ownership on me.*
- *Put his Spirit in my heart as a guarantee.*

But how did we arrive here? Let's trace the story from the beginning....

who God created me to be

God created all things, visible and invisible. Because he is the creator, he is also the rightful owner of all things. In addition to being the rightful owner, God also rules over all of creation; his authority is final.

I am a creature.
Gen. 2:7

God made me.
- *Like a potter, God crafted me.*
- *God made me with skill and intention.*
- *I am complex and complicated.*
- *I have God's life-breath in me.*

I am like God.
Gen. 1:26–27

God made me more than just an animal.
- *I am made in God's image.*
- *I am made to relate to God and others in love.*

©digital planet design

I am known.
Psalm 139; Isa. 42:2-4; Jer. 1:5

God made me and knew me before I was born.
- *God made me.*
- *God knew me while I was still in the womb.*
- *God knows me better than I know myself.*

I am made to be God's caretaker of his creation.
Gen. 1:26–31; 2:15–17

God made me for caring responsibility.
- *I am made to help God in his ruling of creation.*
- *I am made to care for his earth.*

©Christine Glade

I am made to relate to his creation.

Gen. 2:19–24

God made me to relate to his entire creation.

- *I am made to love humans just as God loves me.*
- *I am made to love and enjoy God's creatures and nature.*

I am made for thankful, obedient worship to God.

Gen. 1:28–30; 2:16–17

God made me to glorify and enjoy him forever.

- *I am made to praise God by doing what he intended for me.*
- *I am made to enjoy myself as I enjoy God.*

image of God

In Genesis 1:27, the Bible says, "So God created man in his own image, in the image of God he created him; male and female he created them." What is the image of God? The Bible says that Jesus is the perfect image of God (see Col. 2:9 and Heb. 1:3). However, Christians have understood this concept in three different though complementary ways:

1. The qualities and attributes that distinguish humanity from the animals. Some of these qualities are: reason, will, personality, etc.

2. The ability to be in a relationship with God. This relationship constitutes the image of God in us.

3. The caring of God's creation is what demonstrates God's image in human beings.

It is possible that all three things are involved in what the image of God is. Humans are the image of God because they are able to relate to God, to each other, and to God's creation. In addition, humans represent God in this creation. When humans are reconciled with God, the abundant life that results allows the image of God to come through more clearly.

who i am on my own — when i ignored God and went my own way

Although God made us to be his representatives in creation, humans rebelled and sinned against God. Because of sin, humanity is unable to relate to God, one another, and creation. Death, pain, and suffering entered the universe. Because of human disobedience, the whole creation was thrown into darkness and chaos. Our very existence was in danger. God's amazing grace and endless mercy allowed us to live. However, we live limited and twisted lives. This is also part of humanity's identity.

I was broken.
Rom. 3:10–18

Because of Jesus, I am…
Rom. 6:6; Gal. 2:20
- *I am crucified with Christ.*
- *Jesus' body was broken for me.*

I was a sinner.
Rom. 3:23

Because of Jesus, I am…
Rom. 6:8; 1 Peter 2:24
- *I am dead with Christ to sin.*
- *Jesus' death was the death of my sin.*

I was living my life for myself.
Eph. 2:3

Because of Jesus, I am…
Rom. 6:4; Col. 2:12
- *I am buried with Christ to my old life.*
- *Jesus' burial buried my old selfish life.*

I was a user and abuser of God's creation.
Rom. 1:21–25; 3:13–18; Eph. 2:2

Because of Jesus, I am…
Rom. 6:4; Col. 3:1
- *I am raised with Christ to a new life.*
- *Jesus' resurrection raised me to a new relationship with God and his world.*

I was not living by God's instructions.
Rom. 1:21–2:1

Because of Jesus, I am…
Rom. 13:8–10
- *I am fulfilling God's law in Christ.*
- *Jesus' love for me makes me want to live his law of love.*

God is the solution.

He chose for himself a people, those who would carry his name and be an example to all people. He gave us his word, in which he described his will for humanity and his creation. However, the ultimate solution is Jesus himself. Because he is both human and God, Jesus came to do what no other human could. His life, death, and resurrection created the bridge that allows us to be reconciled with God once again.

The cross is the climax of the biblical story. In the cross, all paths converge; all stories are given the possibility of a new direction. In the cross, God brings restoration, hope, and a new life for a creation groaning for redemption.

I was someone who worshiped my own way.

Rom. 1:25

Because of Jesus, I am…
Eph. 1:12–14

- *I am glorifying God in Christ.*
- *Jesus' glorious victory makes me want to give all glory to God.*

I was a mess.

Rom. 7

Because of Jesus, I am…
Phil. 1:6; Col. 2:9–10; Heb. 10:14

- *I am complete in Christ.*
- *Jesus' perfect work has made my life complete. One day, when Jesus returns, he will make it perfect.*

I was dead.

Eph. 2:1

Because of Jesus, I am…
Col. 2:13

- *I am alive with Christ.*
- *Jesus' new life flows through me now.*

I am…

We live in a culture of extremes. On the one hand, the culture around us emphasizes self-sufficiency and independence over the healthy emotional development of children. On the other, it attempts to bolster children's emotional health and self-worth by constant praise and a sense of entitlement. Both extremes have damaged children who grow up with a broken sense of self and lack of acceptance and love.

A realistic understanding of who we are gives us the chance for a healthy self-regard. The Bible gives us a correct understanding of who we are: people deeply flawed and sinful, deeply loved and redeemed by God, and equipped and empowered by the Holy Spirit to be and do as Christ would.

who i am and who i will be in CHRiST

The story of the Bible does not end on the cross. In fact, the cross opened new possibilities. The goal of the biblical story is not just the salvation of humanity through the gracious work of Jesus on the cross. God desires to redeem and restore all of his creation. The conclusion of this magnificent story is the creation of new heavens and new earth. All things will be made new! In that new creation, God will make things the way they should be.

I am a new creature.

2 Cor. 5:1–5, 16–19; Phil. 3:20-21

- *I have had a total makeover of my mind and spirit and my new body is on order.*
- *My inner self has been recreated after a new model of human being—Jesus.*
- *My body will be made new after the pattern of Jesus' resurrected body.*

I am born of God.

John 1:12–13; Rom. 8:29; 1 John 4:7

- *I have been born into God's family.*
- *I am now a child of God after the likeness of Jesus.*
- *Jesus is the "firstborn" example from the dead of what I shall be in the resurrection.*

I am adopted of God.

Rom. 8:15; Eph. 1:5; Heb. 2:10–12

- *God has selected me to be his child.*
- *I am no longer an orphan.*
- *Jesus is my older brother.*
- *Because of him, I now share in the glory of being God's child.*

I am a child of the promise.

Rom. 9:8; Gal. 4:23

- *I am a child of Abraham, a promised child.*
- *I am a spiritual descendant of the father of faith.*
- *I am called to carry on this spiritual heritage in the world.*

I am Jesus' friend.

John 15:15

- *Jesus considers me his friend.*
- *I am a servant of Jesus Christ, yet he calls me friend.*

I am a citizen of heaven.

Eph. 2:19; Phil. 3:20

- *I belong with all those through history who have loved God.*
- *I am a member of God's heavenly kingdom.*
- *My true identity is with the people of God.*

©digitalskillet

I am blessed with every spiritual blessing.

Eph. 1:3; 2:7

- *I have all that can be had of God's treasures.*
- *I have been given unfathomable riches in Christ.*
- *It will take the rest of eternity to unfold all these blessings.*

I am God's workmanship.

Eph. 2:10

- *I am a work of art.*
- *I have been made by the most creative Artist ever.*
- *I am a poem of God's love.*

I am a temple of the Holy Spirit.

1 Cor. 3:16; 6:19; 2 Cor. 6:16

- *I have God living in me.*
- *I am God's house.*
- *I have been made holy for God to live in me.*

I am a member of Christ's body.

Rom. 12:5; 1 Cor. 12:27

- *I am connected in a living way to Jesus.*
- *I am a part of a living organism bigger than myself.*
- *I have a purpose and function in that body.*

I am sealed.

2 Cor. 1:22; Eph. 1:13; 4:30

- *I have God's royal seal upon me.*
- *I have God's seal of ownership.*
- *I have God's guarantee of a quality product in me.*

I am made pure.

1 John 1:9, 3:3

- *I am made clean.*
- *Christ's life and death purify me.*
- *I am being made holy for God by his Spirit working in me.*

I am loved.

Rom. 5:5; 8:39; 1 John 3:16; 4:19

- *God deeply loves me.*
- *I know this because he has given me his most precious gift—his Son, Jesus.*
- *I know that I am loved because God's Spirit of love is in my heart.*

I am taken care of.

John 6:37; Phil. 1:6; 4:19

- *I am secure in God's hands.*
- *I will not be abandoned; God will complete his work in me.*
- *God will supply all that I need.*

I am victorious.

Rom. 8:37; 1 Cor. 15:57

- *I cannot be beaten.*
- *I cannot be stopped by death, thanks to Christ.*
- *I shall be a winner in the end because God is for me.*

I am going to live forever.

John 5:24; 6:47; 11:25-26; 17:3

- *I will live on with God.*
- *My spirit shall not die but go to be with God.*
- *Even if my body dies, I will live again and get a new body in the resurrection.*

I am in God's planned will as an heir of all creation.

Rom. 8:17, 32; Eph. 1:9–11

- *I am going to inherit the universe with Christ.*
- *I know this because God has given all authority and power to Jesus and I belong to him.*

©Aldo Murillo

the three R's— Reconciled, Ransomed, and Redeemed

Reconciled—to be reconciled means to be united again or to become friends again. Human sin and rebellion caused hostility between God and humanity. However, Jesus united us again in friendship with God by his death on the cross.

Ransomed—a ransom is a price that is paid for release; to be ransomed is to be freed at a cost. The Bible tells us that humanity was held hostage to sin, death and the Devil. Jesus' death was the ransom paid to free us from that slavery and reconcile us to God.

Redeemed—to redeem means to buy back again. Jesus' death paid the voucher, canceling the debt we owed.

a new mind

At the center of the good news about Christ is the transformation of individual lives. Paul tells us in Rom. 12:1–2 that this transformation involves the renewing of our minds. He goes on to say in Phil. 2:5–8 that this renewal is about having a new mindset or attitude that Christ himself had. In other words, we are to identify with and take for ourselves Jesus' whole way of thinking and living.

©Laflor Photography

©debenport photo

meaning of the word "Christian"

In Acts 11:25–26, Luke tells us that believers in Jesus were first called "Christians" at Antioch. The name obviously stuck, but what does it mean? *Christ* is the Greek term for the Hebrew *Messiah*, which means "anointed person." To be anointed in the Hebrew culture was to be set apart for some special service. It came to be associated in the prophetic writings of the Old Testament with God's promised savior of the line of king David— Jesus. The "ian" ending indicates belonging or membership. Christian means "one who belongs to Christ," or "one who is a part of Christ." Therefore, if a Christian is one who is connected to Christ, should it not be apparent in the way we act?

©Quavondo Photographer

who are we?

The Bible describes our encounter with God as a new birth (John 3:3). The apostle Paul extends this idea when he writes that we mature as Christians, and that we must, eventually, give up milk for solid food (Heb. 5:11–14). Just as children need to find their identities, we as spiritual children need to find our Christian identities as well.

Our identities begin with the recognition that we no longer belong to ourselves but to God. That is, we need to recognize that if Christ bought us at a high price, then we belong to him.

In the Scriptures, we learn who we are, where we came from, why we are here, and where we are going. When we read the stories of the Patriarchs in Genesis, we learn how God relates to us, imperfect people who long for him. When we read the Psalms, we learn a vocabulary of praise and petition. This vocabulary gives us words to praise God, to express our grief, and make our requests.

In the prophets, we learn what it means to be God's people in moments of difficulties and challenges, what it means to fail and receive God's grace and forgiveness. In the stories of the apostolic church, we see how the Holy Spirit guides and trains his church to carry on God's mission.

When we make ours the story of God's people, as told in the Bible and in the history of the church, our identity merges with that of God's people. In this process, we grow from infant believers to people mature in the faith. As we appropriate God's story with his people, we learn to teach others how to become part of this great story of salvation.

our identity—who we are,
who I am—depends on the identity of
God's people:

- I am a member of Christ's body;
- I am part of God's people;
- I am a child of God called to love him
  and his creation;
- I am a follower of Jesus because in
  him I am fully alive and willing to serve.

We are able to make this beautiful story
ours only through the life, death, and
resurrection of Christ. Through the Holy
Spirit, we are renewed into the image
of Jesus. By following his steps, we walk
on the path of many believers before us,
God's people, and we clear the path for
those believers who are yet to come.

*Let the peace
of Christ rule
in your hearts,
since as mem-
bers of one body
you were called
to peace. And be
thankful.*

—Col. 3:15

assurance of salvation

What if I don't feel close to God?

Some people feel great joy and freedom from their problems when they first believe in Jesus. But after a while, this joy may fade. This is normal. Sometimes you may feel close to God, other times you may feel distant.

Don't depend on your feelings. The Bible teaches, "If you confess with your mouth, 'Jesus is Lord,' and believe in your heart that God raised him from the dead, you will be saved" (Romans 10:9).

Look for evidence of change. God calls you his child, and has sent his Spirit to work inside you. As a follower of Jesus you should see progress—not perfection—in your desire to obey and please him (Romans 7:14–25). For example, before you became a Christian maybe you lost your temper, lied, or hated people and it did not bother you. But now that you are a child of God, you have a desire to change these habits and you regret your failures.

What if I sin?

Don't be surprised by your struggles. Everyone has them. Every follower of Jesus has certain vulnerabilities, whether it is anger, materialism, envy, gossiping, or pornography. People may persuade you to disobey God, or you may find yourself in tempting situations. The Bible says that before you accept Jesus it is very difficult for you to resist temptation (Colossians 1:13). Even after deciding to follow Jesus, people still struggle with temptation, and sometimes give in to it. The good news is once you've decided to follow Jesus, you will possess the desire to please God daily, and God will continue to help you resist temptation (Romans 7:21–25). No matter what happens, God promises you a way to escape any spiritual danger (1 Corinthians 10:13).

All people sin. When you do sin, it's not the end of your relationship with God. Confess your wrongs to God, and he will forgive you. Find Christian friends and support one another.

What if I have doubts?

Real Christians can have doubts. At times, they may even question whether God exists or doubt some of the claims of the Christian faith. You're not alone. The Bible is full of questioners! Jesus' disciple Thomas said he would not believe that Jesus rose from the dead unless he could see and touch the wounds in Jesus' hands and side. Thomas might have had doubts about Jesus, but he kept his mind and heart open to the truth. When Jesus did appear to him, Thomas exclaimed, "My Lord and My God!" It was his search for the truth that led him into a faith that he had never had before (John 20:19–28). Having doubts and questions may spur you to seek out answers which can bring you closer to God. Doubts and questions can help protect believers from being misled or becoming stagnant and inactive in their walk with Jesus.

Hang in there! When you're discouraged by doubts and failures remember that growth is a process. God has plans for you, and won't give up on you. Ask for God's help. He promises to help you improve (Philippians 1:6).

The Apostle Paul

The Apostle Paul is one of the great champions of the faith and worthy of imitation (1 Cor. 4:16). Paul candidly spoke about his past: a past full of pride and violence. He strongly contrasted the person he was, what he valued and what gave him meaning, with the person he became after his encounter with the risen Christ. His value, his goal and meaning for life were linked to Christ.

Paul before and after

Gal. 1:13–14; Phil. 3:4–6

before, I was...
• born a Jew
• a Roman citizen
• circumcised on the eighth day
• of the tribe of Benjamin
• a Pharisee
• persecutor of the church
• zealous for the tradition of my ancestors

now, I am...
• an apostle of Christ
• an apostle to the Gentiles
• a new person, all of my ancestry and ethnic background is worthless compared to the value of Christ
• a prisoner of Jesus
• a slave to everyone

I have been crucified with Christ and I no longer live, but Christ lives in me. The life I live in the body, I live by faith in the Son of God, who loved me and gave himself for me.
—Gal. 2:20

Authors: William Brent Ashby, BT; Benjamin Galan, MTS, ThM, Adjunct Professor of OT Hebrew and Literature at Fuller Seminary.

Knowing God's Will

What is God's will?

How does God speak to us?

What

Navigating Life's Tough Decisions

Walking through Painful Circumstances

Dealing with Failure

Which way do I go?

When we face the big decisions in life, we often just want someone smarter than us to tell us what we should do. God does have a purpose for each of us, but God is not some big vending machine in the sky or a genie in a lamp that must be rubbed the right way to produce the answers we want. God created us for relationship with himself, and he delights in drawing us closer to him through the questions we ask and the answers he gives.

Warning: There are no easy answers ahead! No formulas or surprises either. God does have some very specific things to say about how we can know his will for our lives. As always, it begins with communication. The better we know a friend, the easier it is to find a gift that will please that friend. The better we know God, the clearer his intentions and desires for us become.

The Right Path

1. Pray to know God's will—but not to give a laundry list of things you want God to do. The One who loves us knows exactly what you need, so ask God to make his will your own. That's a scary prayer because it has the real possibility of changing your life completely, but it's the only prayer that counts.

"Teach me to do your will, for you are my God; may your good Spirit lead me on level ground." Psalm 143:10

Jesus taught his followers to pray: "Our Father in heaven, hallowed be your name, your kingdom come, your will be done on earth as it is in heaven." Matthew 6:9–10

2. Imitate Jesus Christ—this means finding out who he is and what he has said and done. It means living with his words and working on a living relationship with him.

"Be imitators of God, therefore, as dearly loved children and live a life of love, just as Christ loved us and gave himself up for us as a fragrant offering and sacrifice to God." Ephesians 5:1–2

3. Get and stay connected to the body of believers—the church. By rubbing elbows (and rough edges) with others on the same path, we find the nourishment and the encouragement for the lifelong task of learning God's will.

"And let us consider how we may spur one another on toward love and good deeds. Let us not give up meeting together, as some are in the habit of doing, but let us encourage

one another—and all the more as you see the Day approaching." Hebrews 10:24–25

4. Be willing to accept and act on what God makes clear. The Apostle Paul said it best: "Therefore, I urge you, brothers, in view of God's mercy, to offer your bodies as living sacrifices, holy and pleasing to God—this is your spiritual act of worship. Do not conform any longer to the pattern of this world, but be transformed by the renewing of your mind. Then you will be able to test and approve what God's will is—his good, pleasing and perfect will." Romans 12:1–2

What is God like? Is he trustworthy?

God meets our deepest needs when we trust him! 	*"Trust in the Lord and do good; dwell in the land and enjoy safe pasture. Delight yourself in the Lord and he will give you the desires of your heart. Commit your way to the Lord; trust in him and he will do this: He will make your righteousness shine like the dawn, the justice of your cause like the noonday sun."* Psalm 37:3–6 (Written by King David— a man whom God said was "after my own heart.")
When people are cruel and things are terrible, God has big plans: He can take what seems to be great evil and from it create great good!	*"You intended to harm me, but God intended it for good to accomplish . . . the saving of many lives."* Genesis 50:20 (Spoken by Joseph, 20 years after his brothers betrayed him, threw him in a pit, and sold him as a slave. God made him second ruler of Egypt. Joseph saved Egypt, his brothers, and his whole family from starvation.)
When trouble threatens, God's people need to turn their eyes and their attention on God. Praise God ahead of time for his solution—God can turn a terrible threat into a great blessing!	*"We have no power to face this vast army that is attacking us. We do not know what to do, but our eyes are upon you."* 2 Chronicles 20:12 (King Jehoshaphat's prayer as Israel faced attack from multiple armies.)
God forgives our sins. He heals us and redeems our lives from destruction. He sets his love and compassion over our spirits and satisfies us with good things so that we feel as strong as a soaring eagle!	*"Praise the LORD, O my soul, and forget not all his benefits—who forgives all your sins and heals all your diseases, who redeems your life from the pit and crowns you with love and compassion, who satisfies your desires with good things so that your youth is renewed like the eagle's."* Psalm 103:2–5 (King David, listing the good things God does for us.)

God is able to do more than we can ever dream through his power at work within us!	*"Now unto him who is able to do immeasurably more than all we ask or imagine, according to his power that is at work within us, to him be the glory in the church and in Christ Jesus, throughout all generations, for ever and ever! Amen."* Ephesians 3:20–21 (The apostle Paul, at the end of a prayer for believers.)
No matter how bad things seem, God holds onto us—even when we're at our worst.	*"When my heart was grieved and my spirit embittered, I was senseless and ignorant; I was a brute beast before you. Yet I am always with you; you hold me by my right hand. You guide me with your counsel and afterward you will take me into glory."* Psalm 73:21–24
Even when we feel threatened or are in danger, he holds us and can make us strong!	*"So do not fear, for I am with you; do not be dismayed, for I am your God. I will strengthen you and help you; I will uphold you with my righteous right hand."* Isaiah 41:10 (God's words to Isaiah, a prophet in constant danger from the rulers of his day who didn't like the message from God he delivered to them.)
Jesus promises us life at its best—an incredibly good life that last forever, secure in him.	*"I have come that they might have life, and have it to the full. I am the good shepherd; the good shepherd lays down his life for the sheep.... My sheep listen to my voice; I know them, and they follow me. I give them eternal life, and they shall never perish; no one can snatch them out of my hand."* John 10:10–11, 27–28 (Jesus' words.)
God can bring good out of anything—and he's proven that he's on your side!	*"And we know that in all things, God works for the good of those who love him, who have been called according to his purpose.... If God is for us, who can be against us? He who did not spare his own Son, but gave him up for us all—how will he not also, along with him, graciously give us all things?"* Romans 8:28, 31–32 (Paul, who had once despised Jesus and persecuted believers.)

What does God say about me?

If I have joined God's family and belong to Christ, the Bible tells me:

I am chosen and loved by God; therefore, I am loved more deeply than I can imagine ! (Colossians 3:12; 1 John 3:1)

I am forgiven of sin; therefore, God will continue to restore me when I repent. (1 John 1:9)

I am at peace with God, my Father; therefore, I can have peace in any situation. (Romans 5:1; John 14:27)

I am God's own child; therefore, I have a new family. (John 1:12, Ephesians 1:5)

I am God's own creative work of art; therefore, I can be glad and grateful for the person God has made me to be. (Ephesians 2:10)

I am a new creation; therefore, I am no longer a slave to old ways of thinking. (2 Corinthians 5:17; Romans 6:5–7)

I am a citizen of heaven; therefore, this world is not the end. I have a divine destination! (Philippians 3:20)

I am a child of the light; therefore, my heavenly Father is pleased as he watches me becoming more like Jesus. (Ephesians 5:8–10)

I am part of a royal priesthood and a nation that belongs to God; therefore, what the world says about me is not God's opinion of who I am. (1 Peter 2:9)

I am reconciled to God and I display God's reconciliation to others; therefore, I have a valuable role to play in God's work here on earth. (2 Corinthians 5:18–19)

I am able to give my worries to God, because he cares about me; therefore, I can rest in knowing that he will do what is best for me. (1 Peter 5:7)

God is for me, on my side, in my corner; therefore, nothing or no one can overcome the power of my Father! (Romans 8:31)

God is working everything in my life for my good and for his glory; therefore, when I am confused by circumstances, I trust his loving promise. (Romans 8:28)

God has prepared good things for me to do; therefore, I have important work to do—God has made me a part of his family business! (Ephesians 2:10)

What is God's will for me?

What the Bible says

The Bible contains many clear commands for us to follow, but here are a few that refer specifically to doing "God's will" just to get you started.

"It is God's will that you should be sanctified." **1 Thessalonians 4:3**
God wants us to become more like Jesus every day—in our thoughts, our words and our deeds. But he doesn't expect us to do that on our own (Philippians 2:13).

"Be joyful always; pray continually; give thanks in all circumstances, for this is God's will for you in Christ Jesus."
1 Thessalonians 5:16–18
God wants his children to be joyful, thankful, and prayerful people—even when the outward circumstances seem impossible (Ephesians 5:15–21).

"For it is God's will that by doing good you should silence the ignorant talk of foolish men." **1 Peter 2:15**

> "God uses suffering to call us into the peace of His presence. If God could not use pain and suffering for our good, then He would not allow such things to remain in the world.
>
> "The grain of wheat must lie in the dark womb of the earth before it can be called forth into the open air by the light and the warmth of the sun. Then it grows into a healthy plant and bears fruit. God has no joy in our pain, but He sometimes uses pain and suffering as bitter medicines for the treatment of souls."
>
> —SUNDAR SINGH
>
> *(Hindu convert to Christianity and one of the most influential missionaries of the 20th century)*

There will always be people who say negative things about us. But only by our good actions can we prove their words to be false. Doing what is good is the best way to please God while stopping the gossips (Titus 2:7–8).

"You need to persevere so that when you have done the will of God, you will receive what he has promised." **Hebrews 10:36**
God wants us to keep going and he offers great reward to those who don't give up—even when life is hard (Galatians 6:9–10).

What's the value of walking through painful circumstances?

When things hurt, when experiences come that we can only call "bad," it may not feel as though God wants the best for you. In all the pain, anger, and confusion, it is hard to remember that God loves and values you. He has great plans for you and does not want to destroy you!

Good Things that Can Come from Pain

We are "pruned" like a fruit tree so we can bear more spiritual fruit.	*"[God] cuts off every branch in me that bears no fruit, while every branch that does bear fruit he prunes so that it will be even more fruitful."* John 15:2
We can learn to obey God.	*"Before I was afflicted I went astray, but now I obey your word."* Psalm 119:67
We can learn more about who God is.	*"God is our refuge and strength, an ever-present help in trouble."* Psalm 46:1
We can learn to rely on God.	*"We do not want you to be uninformed, brothers, about the hardships we suffered in the province of Asia. We were under great pressure, far beyond our ability to endure, so that we despaired even of life. Indeed, in our hearts we felt the sentence of death. But this happened that we might not rely on ourselves but on God, who raises the dead."* 2 Corinthians 1:8–9
We have the opportunity to become more mature in our faith.	*"Perseverance must finish its work so that you may be mature and complete, not lacking anything."* James 1:4
Our generosity and joy during trouble can bless others.	*"Praise be to the God and Father of our Lord Jesus Christ, the Father of compassion and the God of all comfort, who comforts us in all our troubles, so that we can comfort those in any trouble with the comfort we ourselves have received from God."* 2 Corinthians 1:3–4

"And we know that in all things God works for the good of those who love him, who have been called according to his purpose." Romans 8:28

Sarah worked for Josh—a harsh, demeaning man whose angry outbursts were heard throughout the building. She asked God for strength and help to let go of her anger toward Josh. Ten years later, Sarah was asked to do a job for which she would not have been prepared had she not been trained by Josh. In hindsight, Sarah could see God's good hand in Josh being her boss.

Sometimes God asks us to do what we think we do not have strength to do. God is ready, willing and able to give us whatever we need, if we ask him (Ephesians 3:14–21). He will give the strength moment by moment as we choose to trust him enough to obey him!

"God whispers to us in our pleasures, speaks in our conscience, but shouts in our pains: it is His megaphone to rouse a deaf world."
–C.S. Lewis, *The Problem of Pain*

What do I need to remember about God's leading?

1. God wants you to know his will more than you want to know his will!

You don't need to second-guess God to find out what his will is. God will make sure you know it, whether through his Word, by circumstances, or by other ways. He confirms his will in ways that are unique to your personality, needs, and situation.

However, even after you have prayed about the decision, you may feel tempted to agonize about it. Recognize that this is an "old pattern of thinking," because God tells us not to worry. Then work on changing the pattern: commit your way to the Lord through prayer (Psalm 37:5; Galatians 4:6)—every 5 minutes, if necessary! Rest in God. Be assured that he loves you and is eager to help you!

2. You won't miss God's plan if your heart is set on pleasing him.

Chris believed she had received a call from God to work with Muslim women, but she didn't respond to a window of opportunity because of the difficulties involved. When the window closed, Chris was gripped by a fear that she had missed her opportunity to serve God.

A popular (but unbiblical) notion has circulated in church circles that one might somehow "miss God's will" and be "put on the shelf." The idea implies that a person who missed a window of opportunity can never again be used by God, but must somehow settle for a "less-than-God's-will" life. This comes from our tendency to make God in our own image. God knows all about us—our strengths and weaknesses, our problems and worries. "He who began a good work in you will carry it on to completion" (Philippians 1:6).

Ten years later, the same opportunity presented itself to Chris, and she snapped it up. This time she was really ready. Besides being more mature in her faith, Chris had a great deal of complementary experience to help her in her calling.

3. God has perfect plans for imperfect people's lives.

Bill was a Christian but he was intimately involved with Denise, a non-Christian woman. When Bill's teenaged son announced that he intended to stay a virgin until he got married, Bill said that was great—he  honored it, but it wasn't for him. Yet, over time, Bill's son's comment made him consider his own choices of hypocrisy and rationalization. Bill finally made the choice to end the relationship with Denise and become celibate. During his two years of celibacy, Bill spent a lot of time in prayer. After about two and a half years, a beautiful, bright Christian woman came into his life, and they were joined in a strong marriage.

If God loved and used only perfect people, there would be no one to love or to carry out his plans! God loves us, not because of our perfection or performance but because he is love! Even when we fail him and the people around us, he longs for us to come to him for forgiveness, love, and help.

> ## Psalm 37:23–24
> *"If the Lord delights in a man's way, he makes his steps firm; though he stumble, he will not fall, for the Lord upholds him with his hand."*

"'For I know the plans I have for you,' declares the LORD, 'plans to prosper you and not to harm you, plans to give you hope and a future'" (Jeremiah 29:11).

4. God will give direction to anyone who asks.

You don't have to be a super-Christian to get divine guidance. Many religions claim to reveal hidden wisdom to those who follow all of their rules. God promises to tell you what to do if you ask him, trust him, and follow his leading.

Hannah was struggling with a big life decision that needed to be made very quickly. She went to bed with her mind in turmoil, intending to skip her usual Bible reading in order to pray specifically about the issue at hand. As she began to pray (talking to God, not listening, of course!), the phrase, "Your Word is a lamp to my feet and a light to my path" continually distracted her. Finally, she turned on the light, opened her Bible at its bookmark, and read a passage of Scripture that she understood as a message with particular application to her struggle.

"If any of you lacks wisdom, he should ask God, who gives generously to all without finding fault, and it will be given to him" (James 1:5).

5. God knows the future, so we don't have to. We only need to know the next thing to do.

Melissa was in her 30s, unmarried and childless, with a serious, incurable disease. There were days when she despaired of God's goodness and her own lovability. One day she remembered one of her beloved father's favorite Bible passages: "Trust in the LORD and do good; dwell in the land and enjoy safe pasture. Delight yourself in the LORD and he will give you the desires of your heart. Commit your way to the LORD; trust in him and he will do this: He will make your righteousness shine like the dawn, the justice of your cause like the noonday sun" (Psalm 37:3–6). Finally Melissa was able to "bloom where she was planted," turning her attention and talents to the needs of abused and neglected children in her community.

"But seek first his kingdom and his righteousness, and all these things will be given to you as well. Therefore do not worry about tomorrow, for tomorrow will worry about itself. Each day has enough trouble of its own." Matthew 6:33–34

Relax in the knowledge that we are surrounded and carried in God's loving and capable arms. Only God knows for sure what will happen—and he has already guaranteed to make it work out for good! As one old song says, "I don't know about tomorrow but I know who holds tomorrow—and I know He holds my hand." Focus on doing well today the thing God has given you to do; make good plans, but then let God be God. He is completely able to take care of tomorrow.

6. God is always at work behind the scenes—and he has your best interests at heart!

Sometimes it feels as if God is silent or that our prayers bounce off the ceiling. But during those times, God is putting together circumstances in our lives that will bring the greatest good. He doesn't sleep; he doesn't take a vacation; he is always caring about you and working in your life.

Job said it this way: "When he is at work in the north, I do not see him, when he turns to the south, I catch no glimpse of him. But he knows the way that I take; when he has tested me, I will come forth as gold" (Job 23:9–11).

7. We can seldom choose our circumstances; we can always choose our attitudes.

While working on an attitude may seem trivial when you feel like you're drowning, you are actually giving God yet another opportunity to conform you to his will. When we are in a difficult or confusing situation, he urges us to choose an attitude of faith, of rest, of joy in him (1 Thessalonians 5:16–18).

Psychologist Victor Frankl survived a World War II concentration camp. Life was made as miserable as possible by vicious guards; however, Frankl noticed that some prisoners were happy, shared their bread allotment, and had kind words for others. When they were released, Frankl found that these prisoners had a higher survival rate than those who had focused on the deprivation of the camps. He concluded that no matter what is taken from a person, one always retains the ability to choose his or her attitude.

8. If the Bible forbids it, don't bother praying about it.

God won't lead you contrary to what he has already revealed in his Word. Cheating, stealing, adultery, gossiping, hating, resenting, quarreling, lying, and sexual immorality— these all are already listed in scripture as contrary to God's will.

Before you begin to rationalize ("It's not really as bad as those people say it is"), recognize that obeying God may be difficult. But God will give you strength to do it, if you will choose his way and obey.

9. God's timing is always perfect—not one moment early, not one day late. Give God time to work!

> **Psalm 27:14**
> *"Wait for the Lord; be strong and take heart and wait for the Lord."*
>
> **Psalm 37:7**
> *"Be still before the Lord and wait patiently for him."*

Sharon turned her face away from the friend holding a smiling baby. She had had several miscarriages. Sometimes she wondered if God hated her, if he were punishing her for some sin she could no longer remember. One day Sharon realized she had to choose to trust God in her pain. She chose to trust that he had something in store for her that she could not yet see, could not yet understand. Sharon and her husband Dan became foster parents to a baby, whom they named Joshua. They began to talk about adoption. Soon, they found that Joshua had a cousin a year older who was also available! Now there was a family of four—and a year later, Joshua's biological mother gave birth again. His sister came into Dan and Sharon's family.

In the midst of diapers and tricycles today, Sharon will tell you that trusting God was not always easy. But God was preparing her for this raucous, delightful family she never before could have imagined!

• •

It can be very difficult to sit back and wait patiently when we desperately want to make something happen. Our culture constantly urges us to "do something." In Scripture, God often tells his people to "wait" or to "stand still" and see his salvation. Waiting takes courage to believe that he is at work—and it may be more difficult than "doing something for the Lord."

Henri Nouwen, a well-known writer, professor, and speaker, felt called to leave a life of "doing something" to care for a developmentally disabled man named Adam. Here is some of what he learned as he slowed down and cared for Adam:

"Patience is not waiting passively until someone else does something. Patience asks us to live the moment to the fullest, to be completely present to the moment, to taste the here and now, to be where we are. When we are impatient, we try to get away from where we are. We behave as if the real thing will happen tomorrow, later, and somewhere else. Be patient and trust that the treasure you are looking for is hidden in the ground on which you stand."

What does God do with failure?

God is the God of second chances.

People may tell us that we have ruined our life and destroyed hope for anything good. That is not true. When we are in despair and think our lives are shattered, it is at that very point where God can finally enter in and roll up his sleeves to do something wonderful. When we ask God to take control of the situation, he will walk us through that situation into the next one, and we'll begin to realize that he is always able to do more than we can imagine!

David was God's choice for Israel's king and one whom God declared to be "a man after his own heart." But David slept with Bathsheba, the wife of one of his most loyal army officers. David had her husband killed in battle and married her. God sent Nathan the prophet to confront David and David repented (Psalm 51). God forgave David's sin. Even though the child born to David and Bathsheba died, God restored them and made them parents of the great King Solomon, whose descendant was Jesus Christ (2 Samuel 11–12).

1. No matter what you have done, **God loves you and is eager to forgive you.** All you have to do is ask. Nothing is too big for God to forgive.	*If we confess our sins, he is faithful and just and will forgive us our sins and purify us from all unrighteousness.* 1 John 1:9
2. **God will restore a humble heart.** Accept the consequences of doing wrong. You might need to pay back some money, apologize to someone, pay a fine or penalty, regain another person's trust, or correct a problem that you helped to create. Even if it means admitting you were wrong and feeling embarrassed, these important steps must be taken to fully obey God and learn to live in peaceful obedience.	*He guides the humble in what is right and teaches them his way.* Psalm 25:9

3. Even if you have given up on yourself, **God does not give up on you.** Throughout Scripture, the Lord begs his people to turn away from wrong and come back to him. If we choose not to obey God and go our own way, he pursues us. But he never gives up on us—even when we foolishly insist on doing things our own way and choose to disobey him. He may allow us to deal with the fallout of our disobedience, but he stays nearby, waiting to hear us call. When we finally stop fighting, acknowledge our sin and call out to him, he comes with open arms to give us what we need most—himself.

"Don't just tear your clothes to show how sad you are. Let your hearts be broken. Return to the Lord your God. He is gracious. He is tender and kind. He is slow to get angry. He is full of love. He takes pity on you. He won't destroy you."
Joel 2:13 (NIrV)

UNDER CONSTRUCTION

4. God may change a painful situation quickly; however, **his goal for you is to sanctify you**—to make you like Jesus—developing you into a loving, giving, mature person. These lifelong changes take time. The Christian life is much more like running a marathon than it is like sprinting a short distance. This life is the process that prepares us for the next one. So settle in for the long haul—when you fall down, get back up and keep running—even if you limp for a while.

"Therefore, since we are surrounded by such a great cloud of witnesses, let us throw off everything that hinders and the sin that so easily entangles, and let us run with perseverance the race marked out for us. Let us fix our eyes on Jesus, the author and perfecter of our faith."
Hebrews 12:1–2

5. **God invests time and effort to find lost people.** If you have lost your way in life and have gone in the wrong direction, there is good news—God is looking for you! He considers you too valuable to lose. Don't push him away when he calls to you.

"If a man owns a hundred sheep, and one of them wanders away, will he not leave the ninety-nine on the hills and go to look for the one that wandered off? And if he finds it, I tell you the truth, he is happier about that one sheep than about the ninety-nine that did not wander off. In the same way your Father in heaven is not willing that any of these little ones should be lost." Matthew 18:12–14

Hudson Taylor (pioneer missionary) used to say, "Man's extremity [being at the end of our rope] is God's opportunity."

Life-destroying lies that keep us from knowing God's will ... and some truths to ponder

The Lie: God is punishing me. **The Truth:** Everyone suffers sometimes. God lets us suffer to make us more mature.	*"During the days of Jesus' life on earth, he offered up prayers and petitions with loud cries and tears to the one who could save him from death, and he was heard because of his reverent submission. Although he was a son, he learned obedience from what he suffered and, once made perfect, he became the source of eternal salvation for all who obey him."* Hebrews 5:7–9
The Lie: God can never use me again; I'm disqualified for God's purposes. **The Truth:** Satan loves to tell this lie because he wants you to give up. Remember that he comes to kill, steal and destroy (John 10:9) but God is always ready to forgive. It doesn't matter how bad your life has been—if you give the failures to God, he will use you in a new way.	*"I remember my affliction and my wandering, the bitterness and the gall. I well remember them, and my soul is downcast within me. Yet this I call to mind and therefore I have hope: Because of the Lord's great love we are not consumed, for his compassions never fail. They are new every morning; great is your faithfulness. I say to myself, "The Lord is my portion; therefore I will wait for him."* Lamentations 3:19–24
The Lie: God is fed up with me. **The Truth:** God is not like a human. He does not hold a grudge. His love for you is everlasting!	*"...being confident of this, that he who began a good work in you will carry it on to completion until the day of Christ Jesus."* Philippians 1:6
The Lie: I'll never be happy again. **The Truth:** When you have suffered a tragedy, you may feel as though hope is gone. But, in time, God will fill you with hope, joy and peace—as you trust in him! His desire is for you to overflow with hope. He already gave you the power to do so, by His Spirit!	*"May the God of hope fill you with all joy and peace as you trust in him, so that you may overflow with hope by the power of the Holy Spirit."* Romans 15:13

Words of Comfort and Strength When You Are...

Afraid

I will never leave you nor forsake you. — *Joshua 1:5*

Who knows but that you have come to royal position for such a time as this?
— *Esther 4:14*

We trust in the name of the LORD our God. — *Psalm 20:7*

Though I walk through the valley of the shadow of death, I will fear no evil. — *Psalm 23*

The LORD is my light and my salvation — whom shall I fear? — *Psalm 27:1*

In God I trust; I will not be afraid. — *Psalm 56:11*

Do not fret because of evil men or be envious of the wicked, for the evil man has no future hope, and the lamp of the wicked will be snuffed out. — *Proverbs 24:19–20*

I am the LORD your God who takes hold of your right hand and says to you, Do not fear; I will help you. — *Isaiah 41:13*

Fear not, for I have redeemed you; I have summoned you by name. — *Isaiah 43:1*

The LORD your God is with you, he is mighty to save. — *Zephaniah 3:17*

Do not be afraid of those who kill the body but cannot kill the soul. — *Matthew 10:28*

If God is for us, who can be against us? — *Romans 8:31*

Angry

In your anger do not sin. — *Psalm 4:4*

A gentle answer turns away wrath, but a harsh word stirs up anger. — *Proverbs 15:1*

A fool gives full vent to his anger, but a wise man keeps himself under control.
— *Proverbs 29:11*

Do not let the sun go down while you are still angry. — *Ephesians 4:26*

Be quick to listen, slow to speak and slow to become angry. — *James 1:19*

Do not repay evil with evil or insult with insult. — *1 Peter 3:9*

Backsliding

If my people who are called by my name will humble themselves and pray and seek my face and turn from their wicked ways, then I will hear from heaven and forgive their sin and heal their land. — *2 Chronicles 7:14*

Create in me a pure heart, O God. — *Psalm 51:10–12*

The LORD is compassionate and gracious, slow to anger, abounding in love. He will not always accuse, nor will he narbor his anger forever; he does not treat us as our sins deserve or repay us according to our iniquities. — *Psalm 103:8*

The Lord disciplines those he loves. — *Hebrews 12:5–11*

Come near to God and he will come near to you. — *James 4:8*

If we confess our sins, he is faithful and just and will forgive us our sins and purify us from all unrighteousness. — *1 John 1:9*

Confused

Though he stumble, he will not fall, for the LORD upholds him. — *Psalm 37:23–24*

Trust in the LORD with all your heart and lean not on your own understanding; in all your ways acknowledge him, and he will make your paths straight. — *Proverbs 3:5–6*

See, I am doing a new thing! Now it springs up; do you not perceive it? I am making a way in the desert and streams in the wasteland. — *Isaiah 43:19*

"For I know the plans I have for you" declares the LORD, "plans to prosper you and not to harm you, plans to give you hope and a future. —*Jeremiah 29:11*

In all things God works for the good of those who love him. —*Romans 8:28*

If any of you lack wisdom, he should ask God who gives generously to all without finding fault, and it will be given to him. —*James 1:5*

Depressed

The LORD bless you and keep you; The Lord make his face shine upon you. —*Numbers 6:24–26*

Do not grieve, for the joy of the LORD is your strength. —*Nehemiah 8:10*

As the deer pants for streams of water, so my soul pants for you. —*Psalm 42:1–2*

[The Lord] heals the brokenhearted and binds up their wounds. —*Psalm 147:3*

He has sent me to bind up the brokenhearted. —*Isaiah 61:1*

Because of the LORD's great love we are not consumed, for his compassions never fail. They are new every morning; great is your faithfulness. —*Lamentations 3:22–23*

In this world you will have trouble.... Take heart! I have overcome the world. —*John 16:33*

Whatever is true, whatever is noble, whatever is right, whatever is pure, whatever is lovely, whatever is admirable —if anything is excellent or praiseworthy —think about such things. —*Philippians 4:8–9*

Doubting Salvation

As far as the east is from the west, so far has he removed our [sins] from us. —*Psalm 103:12*

Whoever hears my word and believes … has crossed over from death to life. —*John 5:24*

I tell you the truth, he who believes has everlasting life. —*John 6:47*

I give them eternal life.... No one can snatch them out of my hand. —*John 10:28*

Being confident of this,, that he who began a good work in you will carry it on to completion until the day of Christ Jesus. —*Philippians 1:6*

Envious

Delight yourself in the LORD and he will give you the desires of your heart. —*Psalm 37:4*

Give me neither property nor riches, but give me only my daily bread. —*Proverbs 30:8–9*

I have learned to be content whatever the circumstances. —*Philippians 4:11*

Keep your lives free from the love of money and be content with what you have. —*Hebrews 13:5*

Grieving

[God] will swallow up death forever.... [He] will wipe away the tears. —*Isaiah 25:8*

Blessed are those who mourn, for they will be comforted. —*Matthew 5:4*

When the perishable has been clothed with imperishable, and the mortal with immortality, then the saying that is written will come true: "Death has been swallowed up in victory. Where, O death, is your victory? Where, O death, is your sting?" —*1 Corinthians 15:54-57*

As long as we are at home in the body we are away from the Lord. —*2 Corinthians 5:6*

We do not want you to be ignorant about those who fall asleep, or to grieve like [those] who have no hope. —*1 Thessalonians 4:13–18*

Harmed

You intended to harm me, but God intended it for good. — *Genesis 50:20*

If your enemy is hungry, give him food to eat. — *Proverbs 25:21*

Blessed are those who are persecuted because of righteousness. — *Matthew 5:10–12*

[If] your brother has something against you ... first go and be reconciled.
— *Matthew 5:23–24*

For if you forgive men when they sin against you, your heavenly Father will also forgive
you. But if you do not forgive men their sins, your Father will not forgive your sins.
— *Matthew 6:14–15*

If he sins against you seven times in a day ... forgive him. — *Luke 17:3–4*

Ill (physical suffering)

The Lord is my shepherd, I shall not be in want. He makes me lie down in green
pastures. — *Psalm 23:1–2*

Though outwardly we are wasting away, yet inwardly we are being renewed....
We fix our eyes not on what is seen, but on what is unseen. — *2 Corinthians 4:16–18*

Is any one of you sick? He should call the elders of the church to pray over him and
anoint him with oil in the name of the Lord. And the prayer offered in faith will make
the sick person well. — *James 5:14–15*

Impatient

[God] has made everything beautiful in its time. — *Ecclesiastes 3:1–11*

Wait for the Lord; be strong and take heart. — *Psalm 27:14*

I waited patiently for the Lord.... He set my feet on a rock. — *Psalm 40:1–2*

Be completely ... patient, bearing with one another in love. — *Ephesians 4:2*

Clothe yourselves with compassion, kindness, humility, gentleness and patience.
— *Colossians 3:12*

The Lord's servant must not quarrel.... [He] must be kind to everyone.
— *2 Timothy 2:22–23*

Lonely

[The Lord] satisfies the thirsty and fills the hungry with good things. — *Psalm 107:9*

O Lord, you have searched me and you know me. You know when I sit and when I rise;
you perceive my thoughts from afar. — *Psalm 139:1*

I am with you always, to the very end of the age. — *Matthew 28:20*

You will leave me all alone. Yet I am not alone, for my Father is with me. — *John 16:32*

Neither height nor depth, nor anything else in all creation will be able to separate us from
the love of God that is in Christ Jesus our Lord. — *Romans 8:39*

Suffering

I know that my Redeemer lives.... He will stand upon the earth. — *Job 19:25–27*

The Lord is my rock, my fortress and my deliverer. — *Psalm 18:2*

This poor man called, and ... [the Lord] saved him out of all his troubles. — *Psalm 34:6*

I lift up my eyes to the hills—where does my help come from? My help comes from the
Lord. — *Psalm 121:1–2*

The LORD longs to be gracious…. How gracious he will be when you cry for help!
—*Isaiah 30:18–19*

I will strengthen you…. I will uphold you with my righteous right hand.—*Isaiah 41:10*

We are hard pressed … but not crushed…. Persecuted, but not abandoned.
—*2 Corinthians 4:7–9*

These [sufferings] have come so that your faith … refined by fire—may be proved genuine.—*1 Peter 1:6–7*

Tempted

And lead us not into temptation, but deliver us from the evil one.—*Matthew 6:13*

The spirit is willing but the body is weak.—*Matthew 26:41*

Pray that you will not fall into temptation.—*Luke 22:40*

He will not let you be tempted beyond what you can bear.—*1 Corinthians 10:13*

Because [Jesus] … was tempted, he is able to help those who are being tempted.
—*Hebrews 2:18*

When tempted no one should say, "God is tempting me."—*James 1:13–15*

Resist the devil, and he will flee from you.—*James 4:7*

Tired

The LORD, is my strength and my song.—*Isaiah 12:2*

Those who hope in the LORD will renew their strength. They will soar on wings like eagles.—*Isaiah 40:28–31*

Come to me, all you who are weary and burdened, and I will give you rest. Take my yoke upon you and learn from me, for I am gentle and humble in heart, and you will find rest for your souls. For my yoke is easy and my burden is light.—*Matthew 11:28–30*

My grace is sufficient for you, for my power is made perfect in weakness.
—*2 Corinthians 12:9*

I can do everything through him who gives me strength.—*Philippians 4:13*

I have fought the good fight … I have kept the faith.—*2 Timothy 4:7*

[God] will not forget your work…. [Show] diligence to the very end.—*Hebrews 6:10–12*

Let us run [the race] with perseverance…. Let us fix our eyes on Jesus.—*Hebrews 12:1–3*

The testing of your faith develops perseverance.—*James 1:2–4*

Worried

[He] who trusts in the LORD … will be like a tree planted by the water.—*Jeremiah 17:7–8*

"Not by might, nor by power, but by my Spirit" says the LORD almighty.—*Zechariah 4:6*

Do not worry about tomorrow, for tomorrow will take care of itself.—*Matthew 6:34*

Do not be anxious about anything, but in everything, by prayer and petition, with thanksgiving present your requests to God. And the peace of God, which transcends all understanding, will guard your hearts and your minds in Christ Jesus.
—*Philippians 4:6–7*

And my God will meet all your needs according to his glorious riches.—*Philippians 4:19*

Cast all your anxiety on him because he cares for you.—*1 Peter 5:7*

Spiritual Disciplines

The Classic Disciplines of the Faith:

Bible Reading • Prayer • Fasting

Worship • Service • Solitude

Discernment • Evangelism

What are Spiritual Disciplines?

Understanding the power of sin over us will help us grasp the meaning and necessity for spiritual disciplines.

Sin

The Bible explains sin with several metaphors. Sin:

- Captures (Prov. 5:22; Heb. 12:1)
- Enslaves (Gen. 4:7; John 8:34; Rom. 7:14, 23; Gal. 3:22)
- Is deadly (Rom. 6:23; 5:12; Eph. 2:1)
- Is a sickness (Ps. 32:1–5; Isa. 53:5; Matt. 9:2, 5; 1 Peter 2:24)
- Is impurity (Zech. 13:1; Ps. 51:2; Isa. 1:18)
- Separates (Isa. 59:1–2; Eph. 2:12–16; 4:18)

Sin disguises itself as habits—that is, behaviors and thoughts that have become "second-nature." Many of the sins we commit come so naturally to us that we hardly notice them—whether they occur while driving on a busy freeway, having conversations about other people, abusing substances or other harmful things that may temporarily make us feel better. Habits require time and repetition to become entrenched. These habits enslave us, lead us to deadly consequences, make us sick, corrupt us, and ultimately separate us from God. We have to unlearn many of these behaviors and learn behaviors that are fit for the citizens of God's kingdom.

Spiritual disciplines are practices we do regularly that can help us change, with the power and grace of the Holy Spirit, our sinful habits into good habits that make us more like Christ and connect us closer to God.

Spiritual Disciplines and Salvation

We are saved by and through God's grace alone. We can do nothing to earn our salvation. Spiritual disciplines are not behaviors or practices that make us right with God in any way. They are tools that the Holy Spirit can use to renew our hearts. When we practice spiritual disciplines:

- We recognize that Jesus is the King of our lives.
- We acknowledge that we belong to him alone.
- We also seek to live out the fruit of the Spirit in our lives: love, joy, peace, patience, kindness, goodness, faithfulness, gentleness, and self-control (Gal. 5:22–23).

Spiritual disciplines *do not* help God to make our lives holy. Instead:

- They help us recognize God's callings and promptings in our lives, and identify those areas in our lives that still need to be renewed.
- They make us sensitive and humble to follow God's leading.
- They help us realize that we depend completely on God's grace at every moment and for everything.
- They train and equip us to respond in a worthy manner when life throws problems and storms at us.

Spiritual Disciplines
Should and Should Not Be

Spiritual Disciplines Should Be

- Instruments of God's grace which, through the Spirit, transform us daily into people who reflect Jesus' love, obedience, humility, and connection to God

- Activities that connect us deeply to other believers in our common desire to follow God's will

- A source of humility and dependence on God

- Experiences that enrich our lives and the lives of those around us

© Leah-Anne Thompson

- Activities that occur in the context of God's whole body; spiritual disciplines, although often practiced alone, are not individualistic activities

- As much focused on building up God's body as building up each believer

- Practices that give us hope, despite our failings and limitations. We can hope that "he who began a good work in you will carry it on to completion until the day of Christ Jesus" (Phil. 1:6).

- Practices that permeate every area of our lives

- Disciplines that help us train for the life of faith, hope, and love to which Jesus has called us

Spiritual Disciplines Should Not Be

- Heavy loads of impossible, unrealistic, or unfair expectations for people

- Benchmarks to judge people's Christianity or maturity

- Individualistic attempts to be holy or perfect

- A measure of one's spiritual stature and strength

- A way to separate our "religiosity" from the rest of our lives

- A way to hide our sins with good works

Spiritual Disciplines and the Bible

Contemporary society is fascinated with spirituality. One can find all kinds of books about self-help or spiritual guidance and practices. How are Christian spiritual disciplines different from those offered in such books? The difference is simple, though profound.

Popular Spiritual Disciplines Are:	Biblical Spiritual Disciplines Are:
For self-improvement	For the spiritual maturity of each person and the community as a whole
For self-realization—the fulfillment of one's abilities and potential	For realization of the fruit of the Spirit in one's life
For self-sufficiency	For dependence on God and interdependence with other believers within God's body
Based on one's own work and dedication	Based on the work of the Spirit in our lives, the support and encouragement of all believers, and the effort of each believer.

His divine power has given us everything we need for life and godliness through our knowledge of him who called us by his own glory and goodness…. For this very reason, make every effort to add to your faith goodness; and to goodness, knowledge; and to knowledge, self-control; and to self-control, perseverance; and to perseverance, godliness; and to godliness, brotherly kindness; and to brotherly kindness, love. For if you possess these qualities in increasing measure, they will keep you from being ineffective and unproductive in your knowledge of our Lord Jesus Christ.
—2 Peter 1:3, 5–8

The Apostle Peter is clear: God has given us all we need, and we must make every effort to grow.

SPIRITUAL PRACTICE

Practicing spiritual disciplines is not easy. Jesus reminded the disciples that believers would experience hatred and persecution (John 15:18–25). Spiritual disciplines help us get ready for difficult moments: moments of persecution, temptation, doubt, and grief.

> "A disciplined person is someone who can do the right thing at the right time in the right way with the right spirit."
>
> —John Ortberg, *The Life You've Always Wanted: Spiritual Disciplines for Ordinary People*

Moreover, spiritual disciplines help us to deepen our relationship with God. God does not wish a shallow, "good morning–see you later," type of relationship. God wishes to be in deep, satisfying, loving, transforming, and challenging relationships with us, individually and as a community of believers. Spiritual disciplines build in us the attitudes, emotions, thoughts, and actions that will promote the kind of relationship that our hearts yearn for.

Below is a list of common spiritual practices, by no means comprehensive, which many Christians have practiced throughout the centuries.

---

1. Bible Reading/Study

2. Prayer

3. Fasting

4. Worship

5. Service

6. Solitude

7. Discernment

8. Evangelism

© José Luis Gutiérrez

> "God has given us the Spiritual Disciplines as a means of receiving His grace and growing in Godliness. By them we place ourselves before God for Him to work in us."
>
> —Donald S. Whitney, *Spiritual Disciplines for the Christian Life*

I. Scripture Reading and Studying

Biblical Basis and Examples

- Moses read the word of God to the people and commanded that it be read publicly
  —Ex. 24:7; Deut. 31:9–13
- Joshua was commanded to meditate on God's word day and night—Josh. 1:8
- Kings of Israel were to study the Scriptures—Deut. 17:18–19
- The longest psalm is a psalm about the value of knowing God's word—Ps. 119
- Paul required his letters be read publicly—Col. 4:16; 1 Thess. 5:27
- Paul urged Timothy to study the Word of God and handle it with care—2 Tim. 2:15
- The Ethiopian was reading God's Word and he became a follower of Jesus—Acts 8:27–40
- Jesus read the Bible and taught it to the people—Luke 4:16–21
- Jesus said the value of studying the Bible was to see that it spoke about him—John 5:39
- God's word is supposed to be close to the mouths and hearts of believers—Deut. 30:11–14; 32:47; Ps. 1:2; Rom. 10:8–11; Col. 3:16

The Disciplines Today

Jesus said: "I am the vine; you are the branches. If a man remains in me and I in him, he will bear much fruit; apart from me you can do nothing" (John 15:5).

- Reading the Bible is the best way to stay connected to God.
- Scripture reading is the lifeblood of the church. The Bible equips, trains, and empowers believers to fulfill God's calling (2 Tim. 3:17; 2 Peter 1:3–11; Heb. 13:21).
- Scripture reading and studying involves different activities: memorization, reflection, and transformative study.

Memorization

- ▲ When scuba divers face problems under water, they rely on their previous training to find a way out. When we face temptation or sudden grief, our "training" will kick in.
- ▲ All those verses we have memorized will come back; God will speak to us through them in unexpected ways.
- ▲ One of the best ways to memorize something is by finding partners who help and challenge you to work together.

Reflection

- ▲ It is often called *meditation*. It means that we allow the Bible to settle in our minds and hearts.

- We do this by thinking about it all day long, wondering what a passage or a verse means for us throughout the day's activities.
  - ▲ Write a verse, or passage, on a small piece of paper and carry it along with you. If you are standing in line, waiting at a restaurant, or another short moment, take the paper out and think about how the text connects to your life at that specific moment.

Transformative Study

- ▲ Studying the Bible does not mean one becomes an expert in one passage or book. Studying the Bible means we dig deeply so we can be deeply transformed.
- ▲ The more we know about God, the more we can love him.
- ▲ God gave the Bible to the church. Reading and studying the Bible in community is most profitable.
- Traditionally, Christians have practiced this discipline by reading early in the morning, after meals, or before going to bed.
- Today there are many other opportunities for Bible reading, memorizing, and studying.
- The many hours we spend in transportation can be useful for listening to an audio recording of the Bible.
- The Internet is full of tools and helps for Bible reading and studying.

2. Prayer

Biblical Basis and Examples

- Many of the Psalms are prayers—for example, see Psalms 10, 59, 83, 86, and others
- The believer is to constantly be in an attitude of prayer—Luke 18:1; Eph. 6:18; Phil. 4:6; Col. 4:2; 1 Thess. 5:17; 1 Tim. 2:8
- Access to God through Jesus belongs to the believer—Heb. 4:16
- The manner of prayer calls for honest communication, not showy pretense or empty repetition—Eccl. 5:1–3; Matt. 6:5–7
- Prayer should not be done with an unforgiving attitude—Mark 11:25
- Prayer should be made in confident hope that God hears and knows our real needs —Matt. 7:7–11; Heb. 11:6

The Disciplines Today

- Prayer is commanded in the Bible. The discipline of prayer is a way to be obedient to this commandment.
- Often learning about the heroes of the faith is intimidating. Instead of being motivated, we might feel discouraged with the enormous challenge of their example.
- Who could fly a jet or run a marathon without much previous and rigorous training? No one is born knowing how to pray and being great at it.
- Learning to pray is a bit like learning to swim. It can only happen in the water, despite fears, insecurities, and doubts.
- Prayer requires *concentration* and *focus*.
  - ▴ Teaching ourselves to concentrate is one of the reasons we close our eyes.
  - ▴ But we need to close our ears and minds as well to the many distractions around us.
  - ▴ Spending a few minutes just to quiet mind and heart will help us achieve better concentration and focus.
- Prayer builds up our humility, dependence on God, and compassion for others.
- If praying on your own is difficult, make a "prayer date" with a friend you are comfortable with.
- Start by praying simple, short prayers— pray one minute, take a break and read or sing, then pray again.

- When you feel stuck, unmotivated, or without words—all very normal occurrences—pray a prayer from the Bible: a psalm, the Lord's Prayer (Matt. 6:9–13), Nehemiah's prayer (Neh. 1:5–11), Solomon's prayer (1 Kings 8:22–61).
- Your prayers do not have to be pretty—the Holy Spirit takes all of our prayers, pretty or not, and brings them before God the Father (Rom. 8:26–27).
- Make sure your prayers include, among other things, *praise* for God's greatness, *gratitude* for God's gifts, *petitions* for you and others, *confession* of your struggles and sins, and whatever the Spirit brings to your mind.
- The apostle Paul tells us to "pray continually" (1 Thess. 5:17). Is this even possible? Not immediately. Just as no one can run a marathon without training, no one can pray continually without training.
- Sometimes prayer is a "battleground." Prayer can be difficult and produce anxiety. Sometimes it is while praying that God reveals to us what needs changing, what needs to be done. Sometimes, prayer can be a painful mirror.
- Finally, our prayers are not primarily for changing God's mind about something; prayer changes our mind about who we are, what we need, and how we please God. Prayer is transformational.

3. Fasting

Biblical Basis and Examples

- The nation Israel fasted asking God's forgiveness—Judg. 20:26; 1 Sam. 7:6; Jer. 36:9; Ezra 8:21–23
- The city of Nineveh fasted asking God's forgiveness—Jonah 3:5–10
- Moses fasted when he received God's commandments—Ex. 34:28
- David fasted seeking God's forgiveness and guidance—2 Sam. 1:12, 3:35, 12:16–22
- Ezra fasted to ask God's forgiveness—Ezra 10:6
- Nehemiah fasted seeking God's favor—Neh. 1:4
- Daniel fasted seeking God's favor—Dan. 9:3, 10:2–3
- Anna fasted seeking God's favor and guidance—Luke 2:37
- Cornelius fasted seeking God's favor—Acts 10:30
- Paul fasted seeking God's guidance—Acts 9:9
- Jesus fasted in the wilderness seeking God's guidance—Matt. 4:2
- The manner of fasting is to be sincere, dedicated to God, without a public show—Matt. 6:16–18

> "First, let [fasting] be done unto the Lord with our eye singly fixed on Him. Let our intention herein be this, and this alone, to glorify our Father which is in heaven."
>
> —(John Wesley, as found in the collection *Sermons On Several Occasions*)

The Disciplines Today

- Fasting may be the most neglected of all the spiritual disciplines today. It is easy to dismiss it as an old and quaint practice. But we miss an important and meaningful opportunity for spiritual growth.
- The central point of fasting is training for self-control (2 Peter 1:6; Gal. 5:23; 1 Peter 1:13).
- If we are to break the hold of habits—sin—in our lives, training for self-control is essential.
- Fasting is an effective approach to developing self-control because it deals with a very fundamental necessity of human existence: food.
- We need food to live; however, we can become enslaved by food—or other things we may need or simply want for our lives.
- If we are able to control things essential for life, we will be able to keep in check the things that are not essential for life.
- The practice of fasting fosters humility, reliance on God, compassion, gratitude, and self-control.
- Begin by fasting from food for a short period, such as skipping a meal. Build your fasting time up from there.

- As much as possible, use the time it takes to get or prepare food and eat it for prayer and Bible reflection.
- Fasting from food is the most obvious way to do it. However, you can also abstain from other things. For example, watching television (or other media) often consumes too much of our lives. That central place belongs to God alone.
- If you find you rely too much on caffeine to stay awake or for energy, it may be a good idea to fast from caffeine and be reminded that our dependence on God is sufficient.
- We can extend the same principle to many things around us: technology, music, sports, and so on.
- Internet, although a wonderful tool of communication, can absorb our time and attention in ways not even television could. Try a "media fast." Turning the computer off in order to be completely present in the lives of others has become a wonderful spiritual practice for many people today.

4. WORSHIP

BIBLICAL BASIS AND EXAMPLES

© Peter Brutsch

- Worship must be to God and God alone—Ex. 20:1–6; Matt. 4:10
- Worship must be in Spirit and in truth—John 4:23–24
- Moses composed and taught a song about God to the people— Deut. 31:19–22; 32:1–47
- David danced in worship before the Lord—2 Sam. 6:14–16
- The entire book of Psalms is a book for worship—Ps. 8, 89, and 105 are examples
- Worship may be in a public place—Deut. 16:11; Luke 24:53
- It may be in a private residence—Acts 1:13–14; 5:42; 12:12; Rom. 16:5; Col. 4:15
- Worship may be done with instruments—Ps. 150
- It may be done in silence—Ps. 46:10; Hab. 2:20
- Worship may be done bowing or kneeling—Ps. 95:6
- It may be done upright or with hands raised—1 Tim. 2:8
- Paul tells believers to use psalms, hymns, and spiritual songs—Col. 3:16
- Believers are commanded to worship God regularly—Psalm 96:8–9; Heb. 10:25

THE DISCIPLINES TODAY

- Worship is more than an activity: it is an attitude—an attitude of awe and gratitude, of humble submission to God's greatness and grace, of obedience and love.
- Every activity and every relationship in our daily life can be a way to worship God.
- The spiritual discipline of worship is not limited to the activities we do on Sundays.
- We must train ourselves to recognize God's presence in the smallest of events and in the most casual of our relationships.
- This discipline will hone our humility, dependence on God, gratitude, obedience, and fellowship with God and our fellow believers.
- We can worship alone. However, worshiping with other believers has a way of connecting people in an incomparable way. Worship nurtures fellowship, promotes intimate relationships, and fosters the edification of Christ's body.
- Sunday worship is the best initial training ground for this discipline. As we continue developing this habit of worshiping God, we will see Sunday worship as the beginning of our worship, rather than as the only worship time.

- List your daily activities from dawn to bedtime. Reflect on how each of your activities and your attitudes toward them worship God. Sometimes they do not seem to worship God; is there any way you can make them worshipful?
- Take one event, activity, or relationship at a time and find ways it can bring worship to God. Perhaps all you need to do is dedicate the activity to God in prayer, or change an attitude toward a relationship that is difficult. Perhaps you need to stop an activity or event that does not glorify God.
- Just as prayer can occur all day long in the background of your mind and spirit, worshiping God occurs often unnoticed. If you make a habit of noticing and being mindful about God throughout your day, you will be able to express your joy, gratitude, sadness, frustration, anger, or love in different ways that bring worship to God.
- It is in this discipline that the previous disciplines are handy. You can express your worship through prayer, singing, or meditating on a Bible verse.

5. SERVICE

BIBLICAL BASIS AND EXAMPLES

- Jesus taught that true greatness is serving others—Matt. 20: 26–27; Mark 9:35
- Jesus illustrated the importance of service when he washed his disciples' feet—Mark 10:43–45; John 13:4–17
- Paul followed Jesus' example and taught the same—Acts 20:35; Rom. 15:1–3; 1 Cor. 10:24; 2 Cor. 4:5; Gal. 6:10
- Believers are to follow this example—Phil. 2:3–8; Eph. 2:8–10
- "… faith by itself, if it is not accompanied by action, is dead" (James 2:17)

© David Claassen

THE DISCIPLINES TODAY

- The discipline of service is not self-serving. Serving others to feel better, or to gain people's gratitude, becomes a self-serving activity. We give expecting nothing in return.
- Serving arises from our identity in Christ: we are his servants. Service is not what we do; it is who we are.
- Calling Jesus Lord means that we are his servants. Being a servant means that God called us to be of service.
- One of the ways to serve God is by serving people.
- Service is born of love and gratitude. It requires humility, strength, and love.
- Serving others can be exhausting and draining. One way to minimize this problem is by allowing the spiritual disciplines above to be the basis for our service. In addition, service in community also helps to minimize the problem of exhaustion and feeling burnt out.
- Like the other disciplines, training for service is a gradual process. The more we serve others, especially those with great need, the barriers that stay in our way of spiritual growth—pride, arrogance, indifference, fears, and insecurities—will slowly crumble.
- The practice of service begins by caring for one's own family (1 Tim. 5:8).

- Begin by serving those around you in small and unexpected ways. When they notice your service, be sure to give God the honor and the glory. Enjoy being a faithful servant (Matt. 25:21).
- Find ways to serve those with the greatest need in our society.
- Serving the people we like or feel comfortable with is easy. However, Jesus urges us to serve even if we are treated unfairly or unkindly.
- The apostle Peter (1 Peter 4:10–11) urges us to serve other believers in order to share in God's goodness. Service begins among Christians and extends to others as a way to show gratitude for God's own grace.
- In serving others, we become channels of God's love and compassion.
- When we serve others, we get to see Jesus' heart of love and compassion. Service becomes a spiritual experience beyond ourselves.

"Resolved: that all men should live for the glory of God.

Resolved second: that whether others do or not, I will."

—Jonathan Edwards

6. SOLITUDE

BIBLICAL BASIS AND EXAMPLES

- The prophets Moses, Elijah and Habakkuk retired to the wilderness to seek God's guidance —Ex. 3:1–6; 1 Kings 19:11–13; Hab. 2:1
- Jesus often withdrew to a solitary place to pray—Matt. 14:23; Mark 1:12, 35; Luke 5:16; 6:12; 9:18, 28
- Jesus taught the value of praying in private—Matt. 6:6
- Jesus advised the disciples to retire to a lonely place and rest—Mark 6:31
- The Apostle Paul went away to prepare for his ministry—Gal. 1:17

THE DISCIPLINES TODAY

- We live in a time of continuous visual and auditory stimulation: images and sound constantly come at us from many different sources.
- Often we miss God's voice and signals because we are distracted. We are busy people with busy lives.
- Just as our bodies need physical rest, our minds, hearts, and souls need intellectual, emotional, and spiritual rest.
- The problem with intellectual, emotional and spiritual rest is that they often require solitude and silence. We have grown so used to being surrounded by busyness, noise, and stuff that it is a great challenge to be in true solitude and silence.
- Like all disciplines, the habit of solitude takes time to form. It requires one step at a time.
- Begin by setting apart moments of quiet and reflection.
- Turn the radio off while driving in traffic. Allow that stressful time to be a moment of solitude, prayer, praise, and reflection.
- Solitude can be practiced by setting aside an hour, a day, a week, or any period of time that allows you to focus on God.
- Share with others the insights you gain during your moments of solitude. It will be an inspiration and example to others.

© Brian McClister

"Here then I am, far from the busy ways of men. I sit down alone; only God is here."

—John Wesley (1703–1791)

7. Discernment

Biblical Basis and Examples

- Discernment may include wisdom to understand the times—1 Chron. 12:32
- It may include wisdom to understand dreams—Gen. 41:25–39; Dan. 2:27–48
- It may include wisdom to make moral or judicial decisions—1 Kings 3:9–12
- Jesus told his followers to be wise but gentle—Matt. 10:16
- James tells believers to ask God for wisdom—James 1:5
- Discernment may at times run counter to prevailing human wisdom—1 Cor. 1:18–25
- It is useful to distinguish truth from falsehood and grow mature in the faith—Eph. 4:14; 2 Peter 2:1–22

The Disciplines Today

- Discernment is primarily a spiritual gift. However, all believers are called to be wise and discerning (Phil. 1:9–10).

- While some people in the church have a special gift for discernment, everyone in the church ought to be able to use discernment for at least two purposes:
  - ▲ To understand God's calling and will for our individual and collective lives.
  - ▲ To perceive and distinguish truth from falsehood.

- Discernment develops alongside the practice of all the previous spiritual disciplines.

- At a time when religions and pseudo-Christian cults are drawing away young people and uneducated Christians, correctly defining and recognizing beliefs is key.

- As a spiritual discipline, discernment depends entirely on the work of the Holy Spirit.

- We develop our ability to discern through prayer, Bible study and meditation, and fasting. As we become more sensitive to God's voice and promptings, our ability to discern God's plans and desires for our lives will increase.

- Discernment benefits greatly from the joint search for God's will within Christ's body. We are limited and imperfect beings; we are also skilled in self-deception. We may be convinced that God is leading in a specific direction. However, we could be deceiving ourselves. Having the joint discernment of God's people can keep us from this error.

Discernment: The Spirit-inspired ability to separate our imperfect will from God's perfect will in recognizing, judging, and choosing what is right, good, and pure from what is wrong, evil, and impure.

© Ferran Traite Soler

8. Evangelism

Biblical Basis and Examples

- Jesus charged his followers with the duty of spreading the gospel—Matt. 28:19–20
- The special ministry of evangelism is given to some—Eph. 4:11
- Peter tells believers to be ready to give a reasonable answer concerning the hope of the gospel—1 Peter 3:15

© Kevin Russ

The Disciplines Today

- Evangelism is a command for every person in the church.
- However, speaking about one's faith is not always a natural thing for many people.
- Practicing evangelism as a spiritual discipline will allow many Christians to grow more comfortable in sharing their faith.
- Just like our lives, all the spiritual disciplines are intimately related. They enrich each other and work in harmony.
- Evangelism feeds on all the spiritual disciplines mentioned above:
  - ▲ Scripture study: The more we know God, about God, and God's plans for humanity, the better we can share what God has done for us.
  - ▲ Prayer: Abundant life overflows our hearts and minds. The closer we are to God, the more life we can share with others.

  - ▲ Worship, fasting, and service can open doors to engage people in conversation about spiritual matters.
- We must also train ourselves to be God's instruments. It can be difficult to remember that we are not the ones convincing, transforming, or converting people. That is God's job. Our mission is to share with others what God has done. We do not "close the deal." Only God can do that.
- There are many evangelistic tools and programs that help believers obey Jesus' command to evangelize.
- Often, however, the best way to evangelize is by developing close relationships with people around us.
- Spiritual conversations are most natural in the context of close, intimate relationships.
- A spiritual conversation can be simply telling others your own story about when you first realized the importance of Jesus Christ in your life.

"Evangelism is a natural overflow of the Christian life…. But evangelism is also a Discipline in that we must discipline ourselves to get into the context of evangelism, that is, we must not just wait for witnessing opportunities to happen."

—Donald S. Whitney, *Spiritual Disciplines for the Christian Life*

"There is not a square inch in the whole domain of our human existence over which Christ, who is Sovereign over all, does not cry: 'Mine!'"

—Abraham Kuyper, inaugural address at the dedication of the Free University of Amsterdam

From Bad to Good Habits

© Amanda Rohde

1. **Know** your bad habits.
- Pray that God will help you see the specific areas of your life that need changing;
- Pray that God will give you the courage, strength, and help to face those areas.

2. **Confess** your weaknesses to God with a humble and hopeful heart.

3. **Submit** to God's call to change. Surrender your efforts and receive God's grace. Trust that God is with you and is helping you.

4. **Be accountable.**
- Find one or more people you trust and ask them to pray with and for you about a specific area in your life that needs changing;
- Allow them to be God's instruments in your life for that specific area.

5. **Train** to substitute a bad habit—sin—with a good habit—virtue.
- If prayer is difficult for you, find a person who will pray with you, or begin a praying group that meets once a week.

6. **Be persistent.** Bad habits take a long time to form; it takes an equally long time to break them and acquire new habits.

7. **Be graceful** toward yourself and others.
- It is highly possible that you will experience failure.
- Remember, you are not changing just for your sake; you are allowing God's Spirit to work in your life.
- Jesus gave his life for you. You are that valuable; God will patiently wait for you to get up and continue walking every time you stumble and fall.
- Do not obsess over the actual change; it is not your job. The Holy Spirit is the one who renews and transforms us. Focus on the growing relationship with God. Let God be God and do what he does best: give you new life.

8. **Be grateful** for all the things you already are and have.
- Thank God for every small change that occurs;
- Thank God for every time you get up after a fall;
- Thank the people around you for helping you along.

Authors: William Brent Ashby, BT; Benjamin Galan, MTS, ThM, Adjunct Professor of OT Hebrew and Literature at Fuller Seminary.

Why Truth Matters

10 Common Doctrinal Errors:
False Gospels • False Doctrines
False Gods • False Christs • False Spirits
False Prophets • False Apostles
False Teachers • False Visions
False Miracles

Why Truth Matters

The apostle John once lamented that "many false prophets have gone out into the world" (1 John 4:1). False religions and erroneous beliefs have proliferated in the past two centuries and are more popular than ever. It seems that every year a new destructive cult or bizarre sect makes headlines. A myriad of religious groups, some on the fringes and some in the mainstream of society, offer a bewildering variety of beliefs about God and human destiny. The authors of bestselling books appear on television confidently proclaiming that they have the answers for solving humanity's problems.

What's more, most of these religious teachers and groups claim that their beliefs are either true Christianity or at least consistent with the Christian faith. They talk about God, Jesus, faith, and love; they usually quote the Bible.

How can we know what is true and what is not? How can we determine if someone's teaching or claim is consistent with faith in Jesus Christ? It is not possible for anyone to be conversant with every individual religious sect, book, or teacher. However, it is possible to know the truth that is essential or basic to a healthy, authentic Christian faith and to be able to discern when someone's teachings are not consistent with that faith.

Moreover, the Bible gives us specific warnings about false teachings and the teachers who promote them. In the pages that follow, we will look at ten types of false claims and what the Bible says about them. With some biblical perspective on these issues, we can be prepared to discern in most instances whether a particular claim or teaching is consistent with the truth of the Christian faith. In each case, we will see why it is important to know the truth and avoid falsehood. We will see *why truth matters.*

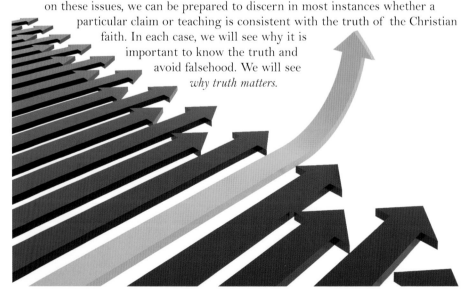

1. False Gospels

The apostle Paul wrote to the churches he had founded in Galatia: "I am astonished that you are so quickly deserting the one who called you by the grace of Christ and are turning to a different gospel—which is really no gospel at all. Evidently some people are throwing you into confusion and are trying to pervert the gospel of Christ. But even if we or an angel from heaven should preach a gospel other than the one we preached to you, let him be eternally condemned!" (Gal. 1:6-8).

THE TRUE GOSPEL: The message that Jesus Christ died for our sins and rose from the grave, conquering death for us (1 Cor. 15:1-4), bringing us forgiveness, a relationship with God the Father, and the promise of eternal life (Acts 26:18; Rom. 6:23; Col. 1:12-14). The basis of this relationship with God is grace—God's undeserved kindness and favor—not our works (Eph. 2:8-10; 2 Tim. 1:9; Titus 3:4-7).

FALSE GOSPELS: Any so-called gospel that presents a different message than the message that Christ himself gave through Paul and the other apostles is a false gospel—it "is really no gospel at all" (Gal. 1:6; see 2 Cor. 11:4). False gospels typically take one of three forms:

▲ SALVATION BY WORKS (LEGALISM): Many religions, such as *Islam*, teach that we must earn eternal life by our good works. More subtly, some religions, such as *Jehovah's Witnesses*, teach that we must be saved by faith in Christ *plus* works. They maintain that Christ's death gives us a kind of second chance to prove ourselves worthy of eternal life.

▲ SALVATION THAT DOES NO WORKS (ANTINOMIANISM): Some people misunderstand salvation by grace to mean that God does not expect his people to do good works. Regrettably, some Christians who have a superficial understanding of salvation fall into this error. They presume that if they mentally accept the facts of the gospel then they are saved and free to go on living the same way. This is just as much a false doctrine as legalism. True saving faith includes an attitude of trust and reliance on God and a desire to please God (Heb. 11:1-6). It results in a life of love and good works (Gal. 5:6; Eph. 2:10; James 2:14-26).

> "If works and love do not blossom forth, it is not genuine faith, the gospel has not yet gained a foothold, and Christ is not yet rightly known."
> —Martin Luther (1522)[1]

▲ SALVATION FOR EVERYONE (UNIVERSALISM): The claim that God will save everyone flatly contradicts the Bible's many warnings about eternal punishment (Matt. 25:41, 46; Rev. 20:10-15). *Mormonism* teaches a form of near-universalism in which everyone except for a very small number of "sons of perdition" will live in one of three heavenly kingdoms.

The biblical gospel is not faith *plus* works (legalism) or faith *minus* works (antinomianism) or faith optional (universalism); it is faith *that* works—faith that results in good works as the evidence (not the basis) of salvation.

2. False Doctrines

"If anyone teaches false doctrines and does not agree to the sound instruction of our Lord Jesus Christ and to godly teaching, he is conceited and understands nothing" (1 Tim. 6:3-4a).

TRUE DOCTRINE: We learn true doctrine from the Bible. "All Scripture is God-breathed and is useful for teaching" (2 Tim. 3:16). The core of Christian doctrine is what Jesus taught to and through his apostles, the truth that sets us free (John 8:31-32; Acts 2:42). Although God does not expect us, in our mortal lifetime, to attain perfect understanding of that truth, he does expect us to learn and understand *sound* doctrine—that is, a healthy, practical knowledge of essential Christian truth (1 Tim. 4:6; 6:3; Titus 1:9; 2:1).

FALSE DOCTRINES: The Bible warns us not to follow those who teach false doctrine (Rom. 16:17). False doctrine mishandles Scripture in one of two ways: either it denies its truth or it distorts its meaning (Deut. 4:2; Prov. 30:5-6; 2 Peter 3:16; Rev. 22:18-19).

"The supreme judge by which all controversies of religion are to be determined, and all decrees of councils, opinions of ancient writers, doctrines of men, and private spirits, are to be examined, and in whose sentence we are to rest, can be no other but the Holy Spirit speaking in the Scripture."—Westminster Confession of Faith (1646)

▲ DENYING: Many people profess respect for the Bible but deny those parts that do not fit their views. Theological *liberalism*, which teaches that most or all of the miraculous elements of the Bible's history are myths or legends, is one of the most destructive errors in Christianity today. It affects most mainline Protestant denominations and many Catholics to various degrees. Theological liberals view with skepticism the fulfilled prophecies of the Bible (typically arguing that they were written after the fact) as well as such miracles as the Israelites' crossing of the Red Sea or Jesus' virgin birth and resurrection.

▲ DISTORTING: Many people also profess to accept the truth of the whole Bible but distort or twist it to fit their views. There are two basic ways to distort the Bible:

↳ MISTRANSLATIONS of the Bible include the *New World Translation* (Jehovah's Witnesses) and the *Joseph Smith Translation* (Mormonism). The NWT inserts the name "Jehovah" into the New Testament selectively in place of "Lord" 237 times to support the Jehovah's Witnesses' emphasis on the name Jehovah and their belief that Jesus is not the Lord Jehovah. Joseph Smith rewrote numerous chapters in the Bible, even adding several verses to Genesis supposedly prophesying the coming of Joseph Smith!

↳ MISINTERPRETATIONS of the Bible accept the wording of conventional translations but then come up with erroneous ways of understanding what it says, often by redefining biblical terms. The New Age book *A Course in Miracles*, for example, redefines *Christ* to mean the divine love that is in all people, *faith* as believing that the universe is on our side, *miracle* as a shift in our perception of things, and the like.

3. False Gods

"Formerly, when you did not know God, you were slaves to those who by nature are not gods" (Gal. 4:8).

THE TRUE GOD: There is only one true God (2 Chron. 15:3; 1 Thess. 1:9), the God known in Jesus Christ (John 17:3; 1 John 5:20-21). This God revealed himself in the Old Testament by the name Jehovah or Yahweh, "the LORD" (Gen. 2:4; Deut. 6:4-5). He has always been and always will be unchangeably God (Ps. 90:2; 102:25-27); no one else has or will ever occupy that position (Isa. 43:10). In the New Testament, this God reveals himself more fully as three distinct persons, the Father, Son, and Holy Spirit (Matt. 28:19), each of whom is truly God (John 17:3; 20:28; Acts 5:3-4). This triune God is the sole Creator of all things (Gen. 1:1-3; Isa. 44:24; John 1:3).

FALSE GODS: We may speak of false gods in three senses:

▲ MYTHICAL GODS: Most ancient societies worshipped a multitude of deities and developed stories about them (*myths*). Some of these deities were imaginary figures, such as *Krishna*, still one of the most popular deities in Hindu religion. Other deities represent various forces or creatures of the natural world (see Rom. 1:25), such as the *Horned God* and the *Goddess* in Wicca or Neopaganism. The Bible warns that demonic beings are the real inspiration behind such pagan deities (Deut. 32:17; Ps. 106:37; 1 Cor. 10:20).

▲ HUMAN BEINGS WORSHIPPED AS GODS: People throughout history have worshipped powerful human beings as deities (see Ezek. 28:2, 9). In modern times, several religions have revered their founders or other men as God in human form, including:
  ↳ *Wallace D. Fard*, founder of the Nation of Islam (a sect rejected by mainstream Islam)
  ↳ *Father Divine*, positive-thinking teacher and founder of the International Peace Mission
  ↳ *Haile Selassie*, an Ethiopian emperor revered among Rastafarians as God

▲ FALSE CONCEPTIONS OF GOD: Over half of the world's population belongs to the three major monotheistic religions: Christianity, Islam, and Judaism. These religions all classically acknowledge that one God exists, that he created the world, and that he revealed himself to Abraham. In a sense, we could say that these religions worship the same God. However, both *Islam* and *Judaism* deny that God is triune (Father, Son, and Holy Spirit). In addition, millions of people, such as Jehovah's Witnesses, Mormons, and Unitarians, accept heretical forms of Christianity that also reject this essential Christian truth.

"We are cruel to ourselves if we try to live in this world without knowing about the God whose world it is and who runs it."
—J. I. Packer, *Knowing God* (1973)[2]

4. False Christs

Jesus warned: "For many will come in my name, claiming, 'I am the Christ,' and will deceive many" (Matt. 24:5).

THE TRUE CHRIST: Jesus Christ was the promised Christ (Messiah) and the Son of God (Matt. 16:16; John 4:25-26; 20:31). He existed before creation and made all things (John 1:1-3; Col. 1:16; Heb. 1:10). Although he is distinct from the Father, the Son is himself God (John 1:1; 20:28; Titus 2:13; Heb. 1:8; 2 Peter 1:1). He humbled himself to become human (John 1:14; Phil. 2:5-7) and was born of a virgin (Matt. 1:18-25; Luke 1:34-37). He lived a fully human life, subject to human temptations, yet without sin (Heb. 2:18; 4:15). He died on the cross, was buried, rose from the grave in an immortal, glorified human body, and ascended bodily to heaven (Luke 24:36-52; Acts 1:9-11; Rom. 5:6-10; 1 Cor. 15:3-4).
He sits on the throne of God at the Father's right hand (Acts 2:33-35; Rev. 22:1-3) and will return to earth to judge all humanity (Acts 17:31; Heb. 9:28). He is the object of the same honor, love, faith, worship, and prayer as God (Matt. 10:37; John 5:23; 14:1, 14; Heb. 1:6; Rev. 5:14).

> "Beware of finding a Jesus entirely congenial to you."
> —An ironic statement by the Jesus Seminar[3]

FALSE CHRISTS: There are two types of false Christs:

▲ FALSE DOCTRINES ABOUT CHRIST: Most false doctrines about Christ deny or diminish his deity in some way. They may teach that Jesus was God's first and greatest created angel (*Jehovah's Witnesses*), one of a group of gods that made the world (*Mormonism*), a man whom God exalted to function with divine powers (so-called *Biblical Unitarianism*), or a prophet whom Christians later wrongly deified (*Islam*). *Oneness Pentecostals* believe that Jesus is the Father, Son, and Holy Spirit and deny that the Son preexisted as a divine person distinct from the Father. False doctrines about Christ also include denials or distortions of what Jesus did for our salvation. For example, for very different reasons both Islam and Christian Science deny that Jesus died (Christian Science maintains that death is not real). Jehovah's Witnesses deny that Jesus rose physically from the grave. Believing such false doctrines keeps people from properly honoring or trusting Jesus Christ.

▲ FALSE CHRIST FIGURES: Many modern religious leaders have claimed to be Jesus or Christ, including:
↳ David Koresh, leader of the Branch Davidians in Waco, 76 of whom died in a 1993 conflict with the U.S. federal government
↳ Marshall Applewhite, leader of Heaven's Gate, a UFO cult that had 39 members commit suicide in 1997
↳ José Luis de Jesús Miranda, leader of Growing in Grace, a controversial movement with a wide following in Latin America
↳ Sun Myung Moon, founder of the Unification Church, which regards Moon as its "Father" and the "Lord of the Second Advent"

5. False Spirits

"Dear friends, do not believe every spirit, but test the spirits to see whether they are from God, because many false prophets have gone out into the world. This is how you can recognize the Spirit of God: Every spirit that acknowledges that Jesus Christ has come in the flesh is from God, but every spirit that does not acknowledge Jesus is not from God" (1 John 4:1-2).

THE TRUE SPIRIT: The Holy Spirit is the Spirit of God himself (1 Cor. 3:16; Eph. 4:30), a divine person distinct from the Father and the Son, yet inseparable from them (Matt. 3:16; 28:19). Because the Holy Spirit works within human beings on behalf of the Father and the Son, he is called the Spirit of the Father (Matt. 10:20) and the Spirit of the Son, or Spirit of Jesus Christ (Gal. 4:6; Rom. 8:9; 1 Peter 1:11). Jesus called the Holy Spirit "another *Parakletos*" (translated "Comforter," "Counselor," or "Advocate"), that is, someone else to be with his disciples after Jesus ascended to heaven (John 14:16, 26; 15:26; 16:7). This Spirit testified to the truth about Jesus (John 16:13-14) and inspired the Scriptures (2 Tim. 3:16; 2 Peter 1:20-21). He convicts people of their sins and opens their minds to believe the gospel (John 16:7-11; 1 Cor. 2:12-16).

FALSE SPIRITS: False spirits may be the spirits of other entities besides God, or they may be false claims to inspiration from the Spirit of God:

> "Inspiration is not a determinative criterion of truth. The question is, What is the source of this inspiration?"
> —Ben Witherington III[4]

- ◢ OTHER SPIRITS: In the New Age movement, many people follow teachings supposedly from various "spirit guides" or transcendent beings. A human who claims to have such a spirit speak through him or her (sometimes called *channeling*) is commonly called a *medium*. Famous mediums include Helena Petrovna Blavatsky (founder of the Theosophical Society), Edgar Cayce (who gave thousands of "readings" in a trance state), Esther Hicks (a major inspiration for the bestselling book *The Secret*), J. Z. Knight (who channeled "Ramtha," the spirit of a 35,000-year-old warrior), and James Van Praagh (a popular TV medium).
- ◢ Some New Age leaders claim that Jesus himself inspired or spoke through them. For example, Helen Schucman claimed that Jesus dictated her book *A Course in Miracles*.

The Bible gives us two basic ways to test spirits to see whether they are from God. The first is to determine if the spirits reveal truth, because the Spirit of God is "the Spirit of truth" (John 14:17). Do the spirits teach the truth about Jesus Christ (1 John 4:1-6)? Do they agree with the gospel as preached by the apostles (2 Cor. 11:4)? The second test is to determine whether the spirits produce or encourage healthy, righteous values and behavior, because the Spirit of God is the *Holy* Spirit (Rom. 14:17; 1 Tim. 4:1-5).

"Inspiration is not a determinative criterion of

6. False Prophets

"Watch out for false prophets. They come to you in sheep's clothing, but inwardly they are ferocious wolves" (Matt.7:15).

TRUE PROPHETS: A true prophet is an individual (1) whom God truly commissioned to speak for him and who (2) speaks the truth (3) about the true God (Deut. 18:18). When a prophet prophesies (or claims to speak for God), what he says must be true, if he is indeed a prophet of God. Anyone can *claim* to be a true prophet (and claim to meet these criteria), but a true prophet will agree with what God has already revealed in Scripture (Acts 17:11) and his claims will stand up to fair-minded scrutiny (1 Thess. 5:21).

FALSE PROPHETS: Bible-believing Christians hold differing opinions as to whether God calls individuals to serve as prophets at any time after the first century. However, they should and generally do agree that at least most of the self-proclaimed prophets in church history have been false prophets. The New Testament contains numerous warnings about false prophets (Matt. 7:15; 24:11, 24; Mark 13:22; Luke 6:26; Acts 13:6; 2 Pet. 2:1; 1 John 4:1; Rev. 16:13; 19:20; 20:10) and not a single statement instructing Christians to accept new prophets that arise.

◢ False prophets commonly claim to speak for the God of the Bible, yet present a radically different understanding of his nature or of the way of salvation:

↳ *Muhammad,* the founder of Islam in the seventh century, claimed to be the Prophet of Allah (God); he rejected the doctrine of the Trinity and denied that Jesus died on the cross for our sins.

↳ *Bahá'u'lláh,* the founder of the Bahá'í faith in the nineteenth century, claimed to be the last in a series of prophets that included both Jesus and Muhammad. According to Bahá'í, Bahá'u'lláh is one of nine historic "manifestations" of deity.

↳ *Joseph Smith,* the founder of Mormonism in the nineteenth century, claimed to be the Prophet of the Restoration. He ended up teaching that God the Father was an exalted Man, that the Father, Son, and Holy Ghost were three Gods, and that human beings could also become gods like Heavenly Father.

◢ Anyone who claims to speak authoritatively for God but makes false predictions in the name of God is also a false prophet (Deut. 18:20-22):

↳ *Joseph Smith* predicted in 1832 that the Mormons would build a temple in Jackson County, Missouri, before his generation passed away (Doctrine & Covenants 82). Nearly two centuries later, there is still no temple there. He also predicted that a war between the northern and southern U.S. states would become a world war (D&C 87).

↳ The *Jehovah's Witnesses'* leadership, claiming to function corporately as a prophet, predicted dates when Armageddon would end wickedness on earth, including the dates 1914, 1918, and 1925.

> "As Christ is the object at which faith aims, so he is the stone at which all heretics stumble."—John Calvin[5]

7. False Apostles

The apostle Paul warned about some unnamed teachers: "For such men are false apostles, deceitful workmen, masquerading as apostles of Christ" (2 Cor. 11:13).

TRUE APOSTLES: In almost all of its occurrences in the New Testament, the word *apostle* refers to individuals whom Jesus Christ appointed to speak authoritatively for him after his ascension to heaven. The basic requirement to be an apostle, then, was that Christ had appeared to the individual and appointed him to that responsibility (Acts 1:21-26; 1 Cor. 9:1; 15:5-8). Apostles and prophets were special offices in the first generation of the Christian church; they were the "foundation" of the church, leading it in its transition from a purely Jewish movement to become *the church*—the international fellowship of Jewish and Gentile believers in Jesus Christ (Eph. 2:20; 3:3-10). What Paul says here in Ephesians 2-3 clearly distinguishes the apostles and prophets from other, ongoing ministries in the church (Eph. 4:11). The temporary nature of the office of apostle is also evident from what the latest New Testament writings say (see #6 on prophets). Those writings urge believers to stay sound in their faith, not by listening to new apostles as they came along, but by remembering what the apostles had said (2 Peter 3:1-2, 16-18; Jude 17).

> "I do not, as Peter and Paul, issue commandments unto you. They were apostles of Jesus Christ...."
> —Ignatius, *To the Romans* (second century)

FALSE APOSTLES: Various groups claim that their leaders are modern-day, living apostles:

▲ The *New Apostolic Church* originated from the Catholic Apostolic Church, which claimed that its twelve apostles would lead the final evangelistic effort before the Second Coming of Christ. When the CAC apostles started dying off toward the end of the nineteenth century and Christ did not come back, the NAC emerged as a movement with an ongoing office of apostle. The NAC claims to be the only true church on earth.

▲ The *Church of Jesus Christ of Latter-day Saints* (the Mormons) teaches that their leaders are apostles. Joseph Smith claimed that Jesus Christ appeared to him, but few if any of the current Mormon apostles make this claim.

▲ The *Word of Faith movement* and some other groups claim that the church needs "apostles" today as part of the restoration of the so-called "five-fold ministry," referring to the five offices in Ephesians 4:11. For example, Word of Faith pastor and author Frederick Price's website refers to him as "Apostle Price" and promotes a video heralding Price as "the apostle of faith."

Note that the problem here is not merely the use of the word *apostle*, but the doctrinal claim that certain Christian leaders receive revelations or exercise authority comparable to that of the New Testament apostles. Thus, describing missionaries as "apostles to" the places where they took the gospel (e.g., Hudson Taylor as "the apostle to China") is a different use of the word *apostle* and poses no doctrinal problem.

8. False Teachers

"For the time will come when men will not put up with sound doctrine. Instead, to suit their own desires, they will gather around them a great number of teachers to say what their itching ears want to hear. They will turn their ears away from the truth and turn aside to myths" (2 Tim. 4:3-4).

TRUE TEACHERS: God has gifted many individuals in the church as teachers (1 Cor. 12:28-29; Eph. 4:11). Teachers have a mature understanding of Christian doctrine and are able to explain it to others (Heb. 5:11-14). Their role is to pass on faithfully to others what they have learned (2 Tim. 2:2). A good teacher will encourage those who learn from him to examine critically, with discernment, what he says (Acts 17:11; 1 Thess. 5:21). At the same time, a good teacher seeks to tell people what they need to know, not necessarily what they want to hear (2 Tim. 4:3-4, quoted above).

FALSE TEACHERS: Not everyone is qualified to become a teacher. God holds teachers more strictly accountable than other believers, because teachers claim to know more than those they teach (James 3:1). Some teachers discredit themselves by trying to teach about the Bible when, as Paul says bluntly, they don't know what they are talking about (1 Tim. 1:7). Such teachers may not be teaching outright heresy, but their teaching is so off-base that Christians should still reject it (1 Tim. 1:3-4). Other teachers clearly deny essential Christian doctrine and instead teach "destructive heresies" that threaten to undermine the integrity of the gospel (2 Peter 2:1). Some notable examples of unreliable or false teachers within Christianity today include the following:

> "A half truth is a whole lie."
> —Yiddish proverb

▲ *Word of Faith teachers*—These teachers claim that God's Word promises Christians financial prosperity and bodily healing, so that anyone who "confesses" that they have these things in faith will experience them. The flip side of this doctrine is that anyone who is not wealthy and healthy has only themselves to blame. Such a teaching discourages many people's faith when it fails to work for them. It also turns off many non-Christians to the gospel.

▲ *Unbelieving biblical scholars*—the media pay a great deal of attention these days to the Bible, but they go out of their way to promote scholars who deny the reliability of the Bible. These include professors who are theologically liberal (e.g., Marcus Borg) or simply skeptical (e.g., Bart Ehrman) who teach thousands of college students every year and whose books are found in every public library.

"A half truth is a whole lie."

9. False Visions

God, speaking through Jeremiah, warned the people of Jerusalem about false prophets who claimed to have visions assuring the people that God would not judge them: "The prophets are prophesying lies in my name. I have not sent them or appointed them or spoken to them. They are prophesying to you false visions, divinations, idolatries and the delusions of their own minds" (Jer. 14:14).

TRUE VISIONS: Throughout biblical times, God gave revelations to his people through dreams and visions. The patriarch Joseph had a dream when he was a boy about his future (Gen. 37:5-10). The apostle Peter had a vision revealing that God wanted Gentiles welcomed into the church (Acts 10). When these are from God, they will agree with what God has already revealed (Deut. 13:1-5). There is substantial evidence that God still sometimes communicates to people in these ways even today. For example, there are numerous testimonies of people in Muslim cultures receiving dreams of Jesus Christ that led them to read the New Testament and accept Jesus as their Savior. Modern dreams or visions that point people to Christ, that do not claim to be the basis for new doctrines or new religions, and that do not contradict or supplant Scripture may be accepted as true visions.

FALSE VISIONS: Any visions or dreams that contradict Scripture clearly cannot be from God. We should view with caution and even scepticism any visions or dreams that go beyond what Scripture says, even if they do not clearly contradict it. This is particularly true of alleged revelations that people promote publicly as messages to the church or to the world, or as the basis of a religion's claim to authority. False visions may include visions—even of Christian saints or the Virgin Mary—when they draw people's focus away from worshiping Christ and instead promote devotion toward the apparition itself. We may classify visions and dreams in four categories: (1) definitely heretical or non-Christian (where the vision or dream explicitly supports doctrine opposed to essential Christian truth), (2) aberrant or misleading (supporting clearly erroneous ideas, though still Christian), (3) of uncertain or unknown validity (where we simply do not have enough information on which to base an assessment), and (4) acceptable and valid (see above on true visions and dreams). Two classic examples of dreams and visions that are definitely heretical include the following:

- *Emanuel Swedenborg's visions*—Swedenborg was an intellectually brilliant scientist and philosopher of the eighteenth century. However, largely on the basis of his alleged dreams and visions, he wrote a series of books reinterpreting Christianity that rejected the doctrine of the Trinity and taught various heretical and aberrant ideas.
- *Joseph Smith's First Vision*—Joseph Smith claimed in 1838 that in the spring of 1820 two "personages"—God the Father and Jesus Christ—appeared to him and told him that all of the churches were wrong.

"Though dreams may play an insignificant role in the conversion decisions of most Westerners, over one-fourth of those [Muslim converts to Christianity] surveyed state quite emphatically that dreams and visions were key in drawing them to Christ and sustaining them through difficult times." —Mission Frontiers[6]

10. False Miracles

"False Christs and false prophets will appear and perform great signs and miracles to deceive even the elect—if that were possible" (Matt. 24:24).

TRUE MIRACLES: The Bible often refers to miracles as "signs" because they are visible pointers to the truth about God (Ex. 10:1-2; Josh. 24:17; Dan. 6:27). Jesus' miracles also functioned as signs in this sense (John 2:11; 20:30-31). Miracles reveal God's power and mastery over the forces of nature, but they also reveal his purpose to save his people. True miracles, whether in ancient times or today, are consistent with biblical truth and point people to the God supremely revealed in Christ (Ps. 77:11-15; Acts 14:3).

FALSE MIRACLES: Although there is nothing wrong with asking God to intervene miraculously to meet one's real need, *demanding* miracles for one's own benefit or refusing to believe in God apart from personally witnessing a miracle shows a *lack* of faith in God (Matt. 12:38-40; 16:1-4; John 4:48). Some people who witness miracles still do not believe (Num. 14:11; John 12:37). On the other hand, apparently miraculous events can deceive some people. The Bible warns us about false prophets who appear to perform amazing miracles (Matt. 24:24). False miracles are often no more than human trickery—akin to a magician's sleight-of-hand (e.g., Ex. 7:11, 22)—but in some cases may be demonically produced wonders (2 Thess. 2:9; Rev. 13:13-14). Christians should evaluate all miracle stories, even those that seem to have good evidence to support them, in the light of biblical teaching (1 Thess. 5:21).

"Whatever men may say, no one really thinks that the Christian doctrine of the Resurrection is exactly on the same level with some pious tittle-tattle about how Mother Egarée Louise miraculously found her second best thimble by the aid of St Anthony."
—C. S. Lewis[7]

- Some of the miracles stories about Jesus outside the New Testament are clearly unhistorical legends (dating from later centuries and reflecting a different culture) that are not consistent with a biblical view of Jesus. For example, the second-century *Infancy Gospel of Thomas* reports Jesus as a child causing a boy who bumped into his shoulder to fall dead!
- Islamic traditions report Muhammad performing miracles, including splitting the moon into two pieces in the sky. Since the Qur'an says repeatedly that Muhammad did not perform miracles (e.g., 11:12; 13:27; 17:59), these later traditions are not likely to be true.
- Various Eastern mystics or gurus have claimed to perform miracles. A contemporary example is Sathya Sai Baba, an Indian guru who reportedly makes small objects such as rings or watches appear out of thin air. These miracles have not been proved or disproved (Sathya Sai Baba refuses to submit his claimed miracles to outside researchers).
- Peter Popoff was a popular "Christian" faith healer who seemed to receive supernatural knowledge of the specific ailments of people in his audience. In 1983, skeptic James Randi proved that Popoff was receiving the information by radio from his wife. Popoff is just one of the numerous fraudulent faith healers in modern Christianity.

Correcting Doctrinal Errors

WHO SHOULD CORRECT DOCTRINAL ERRORS?

- God expects *all Christians* to grow in the exercise of discernment—recognizing the difference between truth and error (1 Thess. 5:21-22).
- One mark of *mature Christians* is that they are more skilled in discernment (Heb. 5:14).
- *Christian leaders* have a special responsibility to exercise discernment on behalf of those they lead (1 Tim. 1:3-7; 2 Tim. 2:14-18).
- The Holy Spirit has *especially gifted* some people with discernment (1 Cor. 12:10).

HOW SHOULD WE RESPOND IF WE THINK SOMEONE WE KNOW MIGHT BE FALLING FOR DOCTRINAL ERROR?

- **Ask questions first**: It is always a mistake to "shoot first and ask questions later." By asking honest questions, you can find out what the other person is hearing or reading and what they understand it to mean (Prov. 18:13).
- **Focus on the majors**: Find out what the book, teacher, church, etc., says about the defining issues of the Christian faith. For example: Do they affirm the doctrine of the Trinity? Do they teach salvation by grace alone through faith in Christ? Do they uphold the Bible as the completely trustworthy, inspired word of God? In some cases, a group will have a doctrinal statement that will give you immediate answers to these questions.
- **Recognize shades of gray**: Although truth and error are clear opposites, most people, even in outright false religions, believe a mixture of truth and error. Acknowledge the good, reject the bad (1 Thess. 5:21-22). Furthermore, some errors are clearly unacceptable within a Christian framework, others are of no serious consequence, and still others are difficult to categorize.
- **Get reliable information**: You might consult a discernment ministry that you trust if you are unfamiliar with the teacher or teaching.

Discernment Ministries

Apologetics Index (www.apologeticsindex.org). Extensive A-to-Z list of groups, teachers, books, practices, etc., with numerous links to resources on each.

Centers for Apologetics Research (www.thecenters.org). International group of discernment ministries; website features an A-to-Z list of groups of concern and where they are located.

Evangelical Ministries to New Religions (www.emnr.org). A consortium of discernment ministries that share common core theological convictions and ethical values.

Recommended Reading

Cabal, Ted, ed. *The Apologetics Study Bible.* Nashville: Holman, 2007. Contains numerous helpful articles and notes on doctrinal and apologetic questions.

Challies, Tim. *The Discipline of Spiritual Discernment.* Wheaton: Crossway, 2007.

Duvall, J. Scott, and J. Daniel Hays. *Grasping God's Word: A Hands-On Approach to Reading, Interpreting, and Applying the Bible.* Grand Rapids: Zondervan, 2001. One of many very good books on how to read and understand the Bible; this one is especially good for those without formal theological education.

Grudem, Wayne. *Christian Beliefs: Twenty Basics Every Christian Should Know.* Grand Rapids: Zondervan, 2005. An excellent introduction to Christian doctrine for beginners.

Endnotes

[1] Martin Luther, "Preface to the New Testament, 1522," in *Martin Luther: Selections from His Writings*, ed. John Dillenberger (New York: Anchor Books, 1962), 18.

[2] J. I. Packer, *Knowing God*, 20th anniversary ed. (Downers Grove, IL: InterVarsity, 1993), 19.

[3] Robert W. Funk, Roy W. Hoover, and the Jesus Seminar, *The Five Gospels: The Search for the Authentic Words of Jesus* (New York: Macmillan, 1993), 5.

[4] Ben Witherington III, *Letters and Homilies for Hellenized Christians* (Downers Grove, IL: InterVarsity, 2006), 521.

[5] John Calvin, *Commentaries on the Catholic Epistles*, at 1 John 4:2.

[6] J. Dudley Woodberry and Russell G. Shubin, "Muslims Tell 'Why I Chose Jesus,'" *Mission Frontiers*, March 2001.

[7] C. S. Lewis, *Miracles: A Preliminary Inquiry*, rev. ed. (New York: HarperCollins, 1960), 170.

Author: Robert M. Bowman, Jr., Director of the Institute for Religious Research (IRR), MA in Biblical Studies and Theology

What the Bible Says about Money

How to Honor God with Your Finances

Bible Promises about Money

Reasons to Give Generously

WHAT THE BIBLE SAYS ABOUT MONEY

Money is a big thing in the world's eye, but from God's view it's a small thing. It's what we *do* with this small thing that makes a big, eternal difference. God cares about our faithfulness with what he has entrusted to us—whether it's a lot or a little. Jesus praised the poor widow who gave generously to God out of her meager income (Mark 12:41–44). Her outward act of exceeding faithfulness mirrored an inward spiritual reality of a heart set on the things of God.

> *"Small things are small things, but faithfulness with a small thing is a big thing."*
> —Hudson Taylor, Missionary to China

Jesus tells us to invest in the kingdom of God so that we will find genuine treasures far better than the fleeting, insignificant riches of this world (Matthew 6:19–21). As we remain faithful to God in our use of money, he will prove faithful to care for us through all life's financial ups and downs. Jesus reassures us with these words: "Seek first [God's] kingdom and his righteousness, and all these things will be given to you as well" (Matthew 6:33).

ATTITUDES TOWARD MONEY

People may have different attitudes toward money based on personal experience or how they were raised. But whatever one's feelings are about money and possessions, they need to be evaluated in light of what the Bible says. Looking at the diagram below, how do you view money in your life?

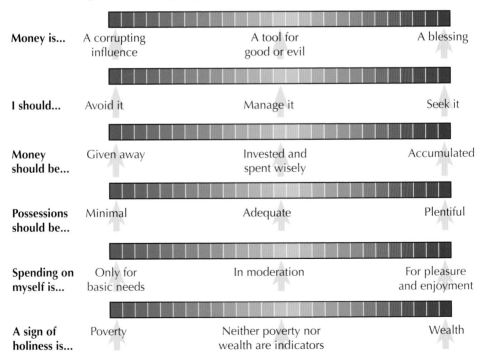

Money is...	A corrupting influence	A tool for good or evil	A blessing
I should...	Avoid it	Manage it	Seek it
Money should be...	Given away	Invested and spent wisely	Accumulated
Possessions should be...	Minimal	Adequate	Plentiful
Spending on myself is...	Only for basic needs	In moderation	For pleasure and enjoyment
A sign of holiness is...	Poverty	Neither poverty nor wealth are indicators	Wealth

FOR THE GLORY OF GOD

First Corinthians 10:31 says, "So whether you eat or drink or whatever you do, do it all for the glory of God." The use of money can be for the glory of God.

God Is the True Owner of Our Money.

In order to use money in ways that glorify God, it's important to first understand whose money it really is. God is the Creator and Owner of all things— including all money, property, and investments.

The earth is the LORD's and everything in it.
—PSALM 24:1

Yours, O LORD, is the greatness and the power and the glory and the majesty and the splendor, for everything in heaven and earth is yours. Yours, O LORD, is the kingdom; you are exalted as head over all. —1 CHRONICLES 29:11

"The silver is mine and the gold is mine," declares the LORD Almighty. —HAGGAI 2:8

Faithfulness Will Be Rewarded.

God is the Owner, but we are his mangers whom he has entrusted with the things of this world. We are accountable to the true Owner to be faithful in our financial transactions.

His master replied, "Well done, good and faithful servant! You have been faithful with a few things; I will put you in charge of many things. Come and share your master's happiness! —MATTHEW 25:23

> *"The everyday choices I make regarding money will influence the very course of eternity."*
> —Randy Alcorn, Christian author

Honor the LORD with your wealth, with the firstfruits of all your crops; then your barns will be filled to overflowing, and your vats will brim over with new wine.
—PROVERBS 3:9–10

Give generously to [the needy] and do so without a grudging heart; then because of this the LORD your God will bless you in all your work and in everything you put your hand to. —DEUTERONOMY 15:10

Whoever can be trusted with very little can also be trusted with much, and whoever is dishonest with very little will also be dishonest with much. So if you have not been trustworthy in handling worldly wealth, who will trust you with true riches? And if you have not been trustworthy with someone else's property, who will give you property of your own? —LUKE 16:9–12

Then the King will say to those on his right, "Come, you who are blessed by my Father; take your inheritance, the kingdom prepared for you since the creation of the world. For I was hungry and you gave me something to eat, I was thirsty and you gave me something to drink, I was a stranger and you invited me in, I needed clothes and you clothed me, I was sick and you looked after me, I was in prison and you came to visit me."
—MATTHEW 25:34–36

God's Agenda Matters More than Ours.

Any money God has entrusted to us has the potential to be used for our selfish ends or for God's agenda. Evangelist Billy Graham said, "Give me five minutes with a person's checkbook, and I will tell you where their heart is." If you want your heart to be set on the things of God, get into the habit of placing your money into things God cares about.

Do not store up for yourselves treasures on earth, where moth and rust destroy, and where thieves break in and steal. But store up for yourselves treasures in heaven, where moth and rust do not destroy, and where thieves do not break in and steal. For where your treasure is, there your heart will be also.
—MATTHEW 6:19–21

But Zacchaeus stood up and said to the Lord, "Look, Lord! Here and now I give half of my possessions to the poor, and if I have cheated anybody out of anything, I will pay back four times the amount." Jesus said to him, "Today salvation has come to this house, because this man, too, is a son of Abraham. For the Son of Man came to seek and to save what was lost." —LUKE 19:8–9

From everyone who has been given much, much will be demanded; and from the one who has been entrusted with much, much more will be asked. —LUKE 12:48b

BLESSINGS FROM GOD

God is the ultimate Owner of all things, but he is no miser. The Bible shows him to be a generous Father who gives blessings to his children because he loves them.

God Blesses His Children.

God gave his chosen people in the Old Testament a land of affluence. Abundance of wealth is portrayed (particularly in the Old Testament) as a blessing from God and considered to be evidence of God's favor.

You open your hands and satisfy the desires of every living thing. —PSALM 145:16

For the LORD your God will bless you in all your harvest and in all the work of your hands, and your joy will be complete. —DEUTERONOMY 16:15

If you, then, though you are evil, know how to give good gifts to your children, how much more will your Father in heaven give good gifts to those who ask him! —MATTHEW 7:11

God Gives Generously So We Can Give Generously.

Our Father's gifts to us are not for hoarding, but for giving as he gives.

Whoever sows sparingly will also reap sparingly, and whoever sows generously will also reap generously. Each man should give what he has decided in his heart to give, not reluctantly or under compulsion, for God loves a cheerful giver. And God is able to make all grace abound to you, so that in all things at all times, having all that you need, you will abound in every good work.... You will be made rich in every way so that you can be generous on every occasion, and through us your generosity will result in thanksgiving to God. —2 CORINTHIANS 9:6–11

Share with God's people who are in need. Practice hospitality. —ROMANS 12:13

Trusting God Is at the Center.

At the core of receiving blessing and giving back generously is our trust in God. Trust is an expression of faith that God will come through for us. It may not be in the way we expect, but he will work all things together for good because of his abundant love.

I am not saying this because I am in need, for I have learned to be content whatever the circumstances. I know what it is to be in need, and I know what it is to have plenty. I have learned the secret of being content in any and every situation, whether well fed or hungry, whether living in plenty or in want. I can do everything through him who gives me strength.... And my God will meet all your needs according to his glorious riches in Christ Jesus. —PHILIPPIANS 4:11–13, 19

THE DANGER OF MONEY

Money can be a blessing used to honor God, but allowing it to become an idol corrupts our lives and harms our walk with God. When we covet and cling to money instead of using money to serve God, we begin to serve money itself.

Serving Money Takes Us Away from God.

Jesus personified money as a rival master to our real Master. Like the rich young man who did not follow Jesus because it meant giving up his money, serving "master Money" will tear us away from allegiance to God (Matthew 19:16-22).

> Still others, like seed sown among thorns, hear the word; but the worries of this life, the deceitfulness of wealth and the desires for other things come in and choke the word, making it unfruitful.—MARK 4:18–19

> No one can serve two masters. Either he will hate the one and love the other, or he will be devoted to the one and despise the other. You cannot serve both God and Money. —MATTHEW 6:24

> Then Jesus said to his disciples, "I tell you the truth, it is hard for a rich man to enter the kingdom of heaven. Again I tell you, it is easier for a camel to go through the eye of a needle than for a rich man to enter the kingdom of God." —MATTHEW 19:23–24

The Love of Money Leads to Destruction.

People who love money will do anything to get it. The grip that money can have over one's life can push one to resort to devious and exploitive means.

> You want something but don't get it. You kill and covet, but you cannot have what you want. You quarrel and fight. You do not have, because you do not ask God. When you ask, you do not receive, because you ask with wrong motives, that you may spend what you get on your pleasures. —JAMES 4:2–3

> People who want to get rich fall into temptation and a trap and into many foolish and harmful desires that plunge men into ruin and destruction. For the love of money is a root of all kinds of evil. Some people, eager for money, have wandered from the faith and pierced themselves with many griefs. —1 TIMOTHY 6:9–10

> By your great skill in trading you have increased your wealth, and because of your wealth your heart has grown proud. —EZEKIEL 28:5

Trust in God, Not Money.

Money's false promises are fleeting and ultimately unsatisfying. God's promises are eternal and always trustworthy.

Keep your lives free from the love of money and be content with what you have, because God has said, "Never will I leave you; never will I forsake you."
—HEBREWS 13:5

Money's False Promises	The Bible's Promises
Security	Command those who are rich in this present world not to be arrogant nor to put their hope in wealth, which is so uncertain, but to put their hope in God, who richly provides us with everything for our enjoyment. —1 TIMOTHY 6:17
Power	So do not fear, for I am with you; do not be dismayed, for I am your God. I will strengthen you and help you; I will uphold you with my righteous right hand.... For I am the LORD, your God, who takes hold of your right hand and says to you, Do not fear; I will help you. —ISAIAH 41:10, 13
Privilege and social standing	People will come from east and west and north and south, and will take their places at the feast in the kingdom of God. Indeed there are those who are last who will be first, and first who will be last. —LUKE 13:29–30
Success	Has not God chosen those who are poor in the eyes of the world to be rich in faith and to inherit the kingdom he promised those who love him? —JAMES 2:5
Love and attention	The LORD your God is with you, he is mighty to save. He will take great delight in you, he will quiet you with his love, he will rejoice over you with singing. —ZEPHANIAH 3:17
Peace of mind	Come to me, all you who are weary and burdened, and I will give you rest. —MATTHEW 11:28
Freedom from consequences	Wealth is worthless in the day of wrath, but righteousness delivers from death. —PROVERBS 11:4
Happiness	Delight yourself in the LORD and he will give you the desires of your heart. —PSALM 37:4

WHY GIVE?

Giving Brings Freedom.

When we release our grip on money, we break free from the grip money has on our lives. Giving keeps us from spiraling down the destructive path of greed. If you want to be free from materialism and the love of money, start by giving.

Be on your guard against all kinds of greed; a man's life does not consist in the abundance of his possessions. —Luke 12:15

Whoever loves money never has money enough; whoever loves wealth is never satisfied with his income. —Ecclesiastes 5:10

What good will it be for a man if he gains the whole world, yet forfeits his soul? Or what can a man give in exchange for his soul? —Matthew 16:26

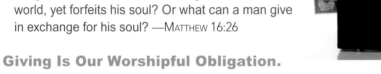

© Mario Aguilar

Giving Is Our Worshipful Obligation.

In the act of giving we worship God by acknowledging that it is ultimately God's money and it is his right to instruct us how to use it. Theologian Richard Foster suggests that rather than approaching the question of giving as "How much of my money should I give God?" we should ask, "How much of God's money should I keep for myself?"

"Will a man rob God? Yet you rob me. But you ask, 'How do we rob you?' In tithes and offerings. You are under a curse—the whole nation of you—because you are robbing me. Bring the whole tithe into the storehouse, that there may be food in my house. Test me in this," says the Lord Almighty, "and see if I will not throw open the floodgates of heaven and pour out so much blessing that you will not have room enough for it." —Malachi 3:8–10

Then he will say to those on his left, "Depart from me, you who are cursed, into the eternal fire.... For I was hungry and you gave me nothing to eat, I was thirsty and you gave me nothing to drink, I was a stranger and you did not invite me in, I needed clothes and you did not clothe me, I was sick and in prison and you did not look after me." They also will answer, "Lord, when did we see you hungry or thirsty or a stranger or needing clothes or sick or in prison, and did not help you?" He will reply, "I tell you the truth, whatever you did not do for one of the least of these, you did not do for me." Then they will go away to eternal punishment, but the righteous to eternal life. —Matthew 25:41–46

And do not forget to do good and to share with others, for with such sacrifices God is pleased. —Hebrews 13:16

Giving Makes Us Trust God.

Stockpiling money may be a sign of trusting in money rather than God. Giving helps focus one's eyes back on God, seeking him as the first priority and relying on him to supply our needs.

And why do you worry about clothes? See how the lilies of the field grow. They do not labor or spin. Yet I tell you that not even Solomon in all his splendor was dressed like one of these. If that is how God clothes the grass of the field, which is here today and tomorrow is thrown into the fire, will he not much more clothe you, O you of little faith? So do not worry, saying, "What shall we eat?" or "What shall we drink?" or "What shall we wear?" For the pagans run after all these things, and your heavenly Father knows that you need them. But seek first his kingdom and his righteousness, and all these things will be given to you as well. Therefore do not worry about tomorrow, for tomorrow will worry about itself. Each day has enough trouble of its own.—Matthew 6:28–34

Giving Is a Fundamental Part of Following Jesus.

Following Jesus requires earthly sacrifice for heavenly gain. Christian author Randy Alcorn said, "The more holdings we have on earth, the more likely we are to forget that we're citizens of another world ... and our inheritance lies there, not here."

And anyone who does not carry his cross and follow me cannot be my disciple.... Any of you who does not give up everything he has cannot be my disciple. —Luke 14:27, 33

Give to everyone who asks you, and if anyone takes what belongs to you, do not demand it back. Do to others as you would have them do to you. —Luke 6:29b–31

I tell you the truth, at the renewal of all things, when the Son of Man sits on his glorious throne, you who have followed me will also sit on twelve thrones, judging the twelve tribes of Israel. And everyone who has left houses or brothers or sisters or father or mother or children or fields for my sake will receive a hundred times as much and will inherit eternal life. —Matthew 19:28–29

Giving is a Privilege.

Whether we have been blessed with much or with little, we can be part of God's plan. Financial giving is one of many ways to do the Lord's work. As God has blessed you, you can bless others.

And now, brothers, we want you to know about the grace that God has given the Macedonian churches. Out of the most severe trial, their overflowing joy and their extreme poverty welled up in rich generosity. For I testify that they gave as much as they were able, and even beyond their ability. Entirely on their own, they urgently pleaded with us for the privilege of sharing in this service to the saints. —2 Corinthians 8:1–4

We have different gifts, according to the grace given us. If a man's gift is prophesying, let him use it in proportion to his faith. If it is serving, let him serve; if it is teaching, let him teach; if it is encouraging, let him encourage; if it is contributing to the needs of others, let him give generously.—Romans 12:6–8a

All the believers were one in heart and mind. No one claimed that any of his possessions was his own, but they shared everything they had.... There were no needy persons among them. For from time to time those who owned lands or houses sold them, brought the money from the sales and put it at the apostles' feet, and it was distributed to anyone as he had need. —Acts 4:32–35

Giving Comes from Love

Missionary Amy Carmichael said, "You can give without loving, but you cannot love without giving." God gave generously to us out of his great love, and we give generously out of our love for others.

This is how we know what love is: Jesus Christ laid down his life for us. And we ought to lay down our lives for our brothers. If anyone has material possessions and sees his brother in need but has no pity on him, how can the love of God be in him? Dear children, let us not love with words or tongue but with actions and in truth.—1 John 3:16–18

Suppose a brother or sister is without clothes and daily food. If one of you says to him, "Go, I wish you well; keep warm and well fed," but does nothing about his physical needs, what good is it? In the same way, faith by itself, if it is not accompanied by action, is dead.—James 2:15–17

PROVERBS ABOUT MONEY

Bribery
A greedy man brings trouble to his family, but he who hates bribes will live. —Proverbs 15:27

A wicked man accepts a bribe in secret to pervert the course of justice. —Proverbs 17:23

Debt
Do not be a man who strikes hands in pledge or puts up security for debts; if you lack the means to pay, your very bed will be snatched from under you. —Proverbs 22:26–27

The rich rule over the poor, and the borrower is servant to the lender. —Prov. 22:7

Diligence
Lazy hands make a man poor, but diligent hands bring wealth. He who gathers crops in summer is a wise son, but he who sleeps during harvest is a disgraceful son. —Proverbs 10:4–5

Envy
A heart at peace gives life to the body, but envy rots the bones. —Prov. 14:30

Fraud
Food gained by fraud tastes sweet to a man, but he ends up with a mouth full of gravel. —Proverbs 20:17

Generosity
He who is kind to the poor lends to the Lord, and he will reward him for what he has done. —Proverbs 19:17

A generous man will himself be blessed, for he shares his food with the poor. —Proverbs 22:9

Hoarding Goods
People curse the man who hoards grain, but blessing crowns him who is willing to sell. —Proverbs 11:26

Honesty in Business
The wicked man earns deceptive wages, but he who sows righteousness reaps a sure reward. —Proverbs 11:18

A fortune made by a lying tongue is a fleeting vapor and a deadly snare. —Proverbs 21:6

Moderation
Do not wear yourself out to get rich; have the wisdom to show restraint. —Proverbs 23:4

Patience
Dishonest money dwindles away, but he who gathers money little by little makes it grow. —Proverbs 13:11

Reputation
A good name is more desirable than great riches; to be esteemed is better than silver or gold. —Proverbs 22:1

Stinginess
A stingy man is eager to get rich and is unaware that poverty awaits him. —Proverbs 28:22

Success
Humility and the fear of the Lord bring wealth and honor and life. —Prov. 22:4

Whoever trusts in his riches will fall, but the righteous will thrive like a green leaf. —Proverbs 11:28

True Wealth
How much better to get wisdom than gold, to choose understanding rather than silver! —Proverbs 16:16

Work
He who works his land will have abundant food, but he who chases fantasies lacks judgment. —Proverbs 12:11

HOW TO HONOR GOD WITH MONEY

1. Ask God to help you depend on him instead of money.

You say, "I am rich; I have acquired wealth and do not need a thing." But you do not realize that you are wretched, pitiful, poor, blind and naked. I counsel you to buy from me gold refined in the fire, so you can become rich.... Those whom I love I rebuke and discipline. So be earnest, and repent. Here I am! I stand at the door and knock. If anyone hears my voice and opens the door, I will come in and eat with him, and he with me. To him who overcomes, I will give the right to sit with me on my throne. —Revelation 3:17–21a

But remember the Lord your God, for it is he who gives you the ability to produce wealth. —Deuteronomy 8:18a

2. Stay focused on what matters most.

Better a little with the fear of the Lord than great wealth with turmoil. Better a meal of vegetables where there is love than a fattened calf with hatred. —Proverbs 15:16–17

Jesus replied: "Love the Lord your God with all your heart and with all your soul and with all your mind. This is the first and greatest commandment. And the second is like it: Love your neighbor as yourself." —Matthew 22:37–39

3. Remember that God is always faithful.

He who did not spare his own Son, but gave him up for us all—how will he not also, along with him, graciously give us all things? —Romans 8:32

"For I know the plans I have for you," declares the Lord, "plans to prosper you and not to harm you, plans to give you hope and a future." —Jeremiah 29:11

4. Ask God for your needs.

Give me neither poverty nor riches, but give me only my daily bread. Otherwise, I may have too much and disown you and say, "Who is the Lord?" Or I may become poor and steal, and so dishonor the name of my God. —Proverbs 30:8–9

5. Ask for wisdom in financial matters.

If any of you lacks wisdom, he should ask
God, who gives generously to all without
finding fault, and it will be given to him.
—James 1:5

© Voronin76

6. Handle money honestly and responsibly.

Give everyone what you owe him: If you
owe taxes, pay taxes; if revenue, then
revenue; if respect, then respect;
if honor, then honor. —Romans 13:7

7. Put your money to work for God's purposes.

Sell your possessions and give to the poor. Provide purses for yourselves that
will not wear out, a treasure in heaven that will not be exhausted, where no
thief comes near and no moth destroys. —Luke 12:33

8. Be ready to give freely.

If there is a poor man among your brothers in any of the towns of the land that
the Lord your God is giving you, do not be hardhearted or tightfisted toward
your poor brother. —Deuteronomy 15:7

9. Practice being content with what you have.

But godliness with contentment is great gain. For we brought nothing into the
world, and we can take nothing out of it. But if we have food and clothing,
we will be content with that. —1 Timothy 6:7–8

I have not coveted anyone's silver or gold or clothing. You yourselves know that
these hands of mine have supplied my own needs and the needs of my
companions. In everything I did, I showed you that by this kind of hard work
we must help the weak, remembering the words the Lord Jesus himself said:
"It is more blessed to give than to receive." —Acts 20:33–35

10. Praise God for his blessings!

Praise the Lord. Blessed is the man who fears the Lord, who finds great delight
in his commands. His children will be mighty in the land; the generation of
the upright will be blessed. Wealth and riches are in his house, and his
righteousness endures forever. Even in darkness light dawns for the upright, for
the gracious and compassionate and righteous man. Good will come to him who
is generous and lends freely, who conducts his affairs with justice. —Psalm 112

DO'S AND DON'TS WITH MONEY

Don't	Do
Don't love it! Luke 16:13	Love the Lord. Deuteronomy 6:5
Don't think it will last. Jeremiah 17:11	Only the things of God will last. Matt. 19:21
Don't think it can save you. Psalm 37:16–17	Remember that only God can save you. Psalm 27:1
Don't serve it. Matthew 6:24	Serve the Lord. 1 Peter 5:2; Mark 12:41–44
Don't envy others who have it. Ex. 20:17	Be content with what you have. Luke 3:14
Don't hoard it. James 5:3–6	Remember that God provides. Job 1:20–21; James 4:13–15
Don't be foolish with it. Proverbs 17:16	Use it wisely. Proverbs 31:10–31
Don't think it can compensate for turmoil. Proverbs 15:16–17	Find peace in God. Romans 15:13
Don't rely on it. Psalm 62:10	Rely on the Lord. Proverbs 18:10–11
Don't think it can buy God's blessings. Acts 8:9–24	Find blessings by living for God. 2 Corinthians 6:10
Don't use it for fraud. Micah 2:2	Repay your debts with it. Psalm 37:21
Don't oppress people to get it. Proverbs 22:16; Amos 2:6–7	Work to get it. 2 Thessalonians 3:9–11
Don't steal it. Titus 2:9–10; Exodus 20:15	Handle it justly. Leviticus 25:14; Psalm 112:5
Don't give special honor to those who have it. James 2:2–6	Give it to those in need. Matthew 5:41–42
Don't use it dishonestly. Proverbs 13:11	Be trustworthy with it. Proverbs 11:1
Don't use it for evil. Ezekiel 8:12–13	Honor God with it. Proverbs 3:9–10
Don't extort it. Ezekiel 22:29	Earn it. Proverbs 13:4
Don't be greedy for it. Luke 12:15	Give it intentionally. 1 Corinthians 16:2
Don't worry about it. Matthew 6:34	Know that God will take care of you. Proverbs 15:25

Author: Jessica Curiel, MA

24 Ways
to Explain
the Gospel

Word Pictures to Share the Good News

Illustrations of Salvation

Evangelism Plans

24 Ways to Explain the Gospel

Some concepts and ideas in the Bible are difficult to express in words. Things like love, forgiveness, sin, and others are very abstract and complex. Metaphors make abstract concepts easier to understand. By using common experiences—such as gardening, becoming ill, joining a family, becoming a citizen, or having debt—metaphors allow people to connect with the concepts at a personal level.

The gospel is about the good news of Jesus: Jesus has come to save us. It is important to explore, learn, appropriate, and use the illustrations the Bible itself uses to explain what Jesus accomplished on the cross.

What does "salvation" mean? How does the Bible explain it? How do we explain it to others? The following pages list twenty-four illustrations of salvation in the Bible.

For it is by grace you have been saved, through faith—and this not from yourselves, it is the gift of God— not by works, so that no one can boast
—Ephesians 2:8–9

A *metaphor* is a figure of speech in which a word or phrase, literally denoting one kind of object or idea, is used in place of another to suggest a likeness or analogy between them.
An *illustration* is an example or instance that helps explain and make something clear.

Removing the Veil

The Bible is God's revelation to humans (2 Tim. 3:16). That means that in the Bible we meet and get to know who God is and what he has done. Revelation means that something hidden is unveiled so it is open to be seen. We can only know God if he lifts the veil from our eyes so we can know him and his actions.

- The Lord Jesus spoke about "the secrets of the kingdom of God" (Luke 8:10). The Apostle Paul wrote about the mysteries God revealed to us in Jesus (Rom. 16:25; Eph. 1:9; 3:6; Col. 1:26).
- These secrets and mysteries are now revealed in the Scriptures. However, not all mysteries are revealed (Deut. 29:29). God lifted the veil far enough to let us see: who God is, what he has done in history, Jesus' work of salvation, and our need for that salvation.

Metaphor	**Biology**	Jesus promises us a new and abundant life (John 10:10).
Positive	**Life**	• Abundant life (John 5:24–26) • Bread of life (John 6:35) • God wants us to be fruitful (John 15:8; Col. 1:10).
Negative	**Death**	• Deserving death (Rom. 1:32) • Death through Adam (Rom. 5:12–14) • Sin causes lack of fruit (Gen. 3:16–19; Luke 3:9; John 15:2).
Illustrations		• Death is a human reality. But Jesus offers life, eternal life. • As a metaphor, death represents the end of all possibilities and hope. People live as if they were dead, without hope and separated from God. • Jesus offers abundant life. Jesus offers a new opportunity to live life like God intended it from the beginning. • Jesus raised Lazarus from the dead (John 11). Besides being a miracle, it also illustrates what Jesus can and does for people: He gives new life. • As we receive new life, God wants us to be fruitful and share this new life with the people around us.

Metaphor	**Human Development**	Jesus promises to complete the transforming work of maturity in each believer (Phil. 1:6).
Positive	**Maturity**	• Parable of the Sower (Luke 8:14) • Becoming mature (Eph. 4:13) • Perseverance to maturity (James 1:4) • No longer foolish (Titus 3:3)
Negative	**Immaturity**	• Idols made by humans are foolishness (Jer. 10:8). • In need of teaching (Rom. 2:20) • Ignorance of God's will (Eph. 5:17)
Illustrations		• One of the effects of sin is that it stunts growth. God intended humans to live a full life. Sin does not allow us to reach our true potential. It makes people act like fools, in immature ways. • Sin has stunted our growth. Although we claim wisdom, our sin has made us fools (Rom. 1:22). • When Jesus cares for us, we become like trees planted by abundant waters that have the maturity to stand during droughts (Ps. 1:1).

Metaphor	FAMILY	Through Jesus, believers become children of God and can call him, "Abba, Father" (Gal. 4:6).
Positive	ADOPTION	• Christians become part of God's family (Rom. 8:15; Eph. 1:5). • Have the full rights of a son (Gal. 4:5). • Receive the assurance that God will resurrect believers' bodies.
Negative	ORPHAN	• The orphan, along with the widow and the poor, are the most vulnerable and needy in society (Deut. 10:18; James 1:26–27). • Life apart from God is like that of an orphan: full of uncertainty, danger, and lack of love (Hos. 14:1–3).
Illustrations		• Orphans are some of the most neglected, unprotected, and unloved people in societies throughout history. • Family connections were decisive for survival and a chance to succeed. • Christians call God "Father" because God has adopted us into his family. • The word *Abba* is a close affectionate term like *daddy*. • Now, regardless of who our family is, whether they are good or not, we all have one, good Father.

Adoption in the Ancient World

- Although the term adoption is not found in the Old Testament, the Old Testament does speak about Israel as God's child (Ex. 4:22; 6:6–7; Jer. 3:19) and the Israelite king, as representative of the whole nation, as a son of God (Ps. 2:7; 89:26).

- In the first century AD, Roman adoption practice was common among the higher classes. Roman adoption was final. The adopted child broke all ties with past connections and was given the standing of a natural child, along with full privileges and requirements. Being adopted meant a complete change of status and life.

- The Apostle Paul combines these two concepts: the Old Testament's (Rom. 9:4) and Roman law (Gal. 4:5). He develops the idea of adoption as an illustration of what Jesus accomplished on the cross.

- The reason God adopts people is love. Out of his love, God grants adoption to people who do not deserve it. Only God's grace allows people to be adopted.

Metaphor	HEALTH	Jesus promises to be our physician and heal our minds, hearts, and souls (Mark 2:17).
Positive	HEALING	• Through Jesus' sacrifice, we are healed from our sins (Isa. 53:5; 1 Peter 2:24). • Prayer and confession to be healed (James 5:16) • God forgives our sins and heals our illness (Ps. 103:3).
Negative	ILLNESS	• Sickness (Matt. 9:2, 5; 1 Peter 2:24)
Illustrations		• The common experience of illness offers many possibilities to illustrate Christ's work. • "It is not the healthy who need a doctor but the sick…" Jesus used these words to describe his own ministry. The prophet Isaiah had promised: "No one living in Zion will say, 'I am ill'; and the sins of those who dwell there will be forgiven" (Isa. 33:24). • There are illnesses that our body can fight off alone. There are others, however, that require help. There are personality faults and character issues that one can deal with. There is a deep, moral problem, called sin, that only one physician can cure: Jesus.

Metaphor	RELATIONSHIP	Jesus promises to be more than our master. He promises to be our friend (John 15:15).
Positive	FRIEND	• Jesus gave his life for his friends (John 15:13). • We show our friendship through our obedience (John 15:14).
Negative	ENEMY	• We were God's enemies (Rom. 5:10; Col. 1:21); in Jesus, we are reconciled with God. • Jesus will defeat his enemies (1 Cor. 15:25).
Illustrations		• Sin has created a gap between God and humans. • This gap is enmity between God and us. • Jesus became a bridge that allows us to walk over to God. • Then, we can have a relationship with God as his friends.

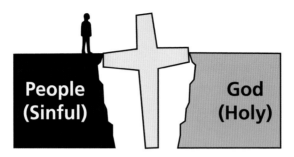

This drawing illustrates how Jesus' work on the cross allows sinful people to begin a relationship with God and be rescued from eternal death.

Metaphor	RESCUE	Jesus promises to rescue and keep us safe forever (Deut. 31:6; Heb. 13:5).
Positive	SAVED	• Jesus came to save the world (John 3:17). • Saves us from our sins (Eph. 2:1–9). • Saves us from God's just wrath (Rom. 5:9). • Saves us from death (Heb. 2:14–15). • Whoever believes in Jesus will not perish (John 3:16). • Jesus gives eternal life (John 10:28).
Negative	PERISHING	• God does not want anyone to perish (2 Peter 3:9). • Eternal Death (Matt. 25:41, 46; Matt. 7:13; Rev. 20:14–15) • Gehenna (Garbage Dump) (Matt. 5:22, 29, 30; 10:28; 18:9; 23:15, 33; Mark 9:43–47; Luke 12:5)
Illustrations		• Jesus speaks of the wicked perishing in "Gehenna." • Gehenna is another word for hell, but it was also the garbage dump of the city of Jerusalem, where garbage was continually burning. • Our sin had broken us and made us useless to God. • We were ready for the garbage dump. • Jesus came to rescue us from the never-ending trash pile. • Jesus' cross stands as a bridge that leads us to eternal safety.

Metaphor	ECONOMIC	Jesus bought each believer at a price; the sale is final (1 Cor. 6:20; 7:23).
Positive	PAYMENT	• Offered himself as ransom (payment) on our behalf (Matt. 20:28; Heb. 9:15) • His sacrifice on the cross paid in full the debt that sin caused.
Negative	DEBT	• Sin caused a "debt" with God—Jesus cancels this debt (Col. 2:14). • The price for redemption is high (1 Peter 1:19).
Illustrations		• Difficult economic times make the burden of debts a very concrete reality. Although we often ignore it, the burden of sin is much heavier. • Getting rid of the huge weight of financial debt would allow people to start over, be wiser, and live better. Similarly, when Jesus lifts the weight of sin from us through his death, we are free to live life to the fullest. Jesus offers the opportunity to live without the burden of sin so we can live the abundant life that Jesus promises. • Another way to understand redemption is when someone buys from a pawnshop. Paying the full price for the object frees it to be taken away.

Redemption

- Redemption refers to the payment one offers for the deliverance of some one or something.

- In the ancient world, redemption was related to the freedom of prisoners of war and slaves. In this sense, God redeemed Israel from Egypt with power.

- In the Old Testament, redemption was a common social practice. As in the example of Naomi, a family member had the obligation to *redeem* another family member who suffered misfortune. To preserve the family honor, the kinsman redeemer (*goel* in Hebrew) would pay the debts to free the family member from her obligations or from slavery.

- A wonderful illustration of redemption is the story of Hosea in the Old Testament. God had commanded him to marry a woman who would betray him. Yet, God also ordered that Hosea had to forgive her and keep her as his wife. At one point, Gomer, Hosea's unfaithful wife, became a slave. God ordered Hosea to buy her out, to redeem her. Once redeemed, Hosea owned Gomer and could have done anything he wanted to her. Yet, Hosea brought her back to his house as his wife again, forgave her, and demanded that she behave faithfully. Christ redeems us because he loves us; instead of treating us like slaves, Jesus calls us "friends" (John 15:15).

- The New Testament uses this metaphor to explain what Jesus accomplished on the cross. Jesus redeemed us from the power of sin and evil. His blood was the price he paid to make us free. The price for our freedom from sin and death was too high for any human to pay. Jesus alone was able to make the only and final payment for our redemption. Jesus' redemption is a free offer to every person.

Metaphor	LEGAL	In Jesus we find complete forgiveness so God "will tread our sins underfoot and hurl our iniquities into the depths of the sea" (Micah 7:19).
Positive	FORGIVENESS	• Sins are forgiven forever (Jer. 31:34; Heb. 8:12). • Forgiveness comes from God's grace (Eph. 1:7). • God desires for everyone to be forgiven (1 Tim. 2:4).
Negative	CRIME AND PUNISHMENT	• A compassionate but just God (Num. 14:18) • God punishes sin (Lam. 3:39). • God is the ultimate judge (Prov. 24:12; Rom. 14:12).
Illustrations		• Most people, at one point in their lives, have had to deal with a legal issue—a parking ticket, a dispute in court, the selling of a home, or other more serious cases. • While not pleasant, we understand that the legal requirements and process is necessary and healthy. • The Bible uses this metaphor to show both the necessity and the rightness of Jesus' ministry of forgiveness and eventual judgment. • The legal consequences of sin are so big and eternal that we cannot deal with it on our own. Jesus is the only person who can and has done something about it. • His death on the cross has made it possible for us to receive God's forgiveness. • The Bible presents Jesus' work as an advocate on our behalf. He is our "defense lawyer" (Heb. 7:25; 1 John 2:1, 9).

Metaphor	MILITARY	Jesus has promised to give us lasting peace (John 14:27).
Positive	PEACE	• Peace with God through faith in Jesus (Rom. 5:1) • Jesus destroyed barriers of hostility (Eph. 2:14–22). • Jesus has defeated the powers of this world (1 Cor. 15:24–28). • Believers are also victorious (Rom. 8:31–39).
Negative	WAR	• We were God's enemies (Rom. 5:10; Col. 1:21). • We were under the dominion of darkness (Col. 1:12–14). • We were followers of the Devil and his ways (Eph. 2:1–7).
Illustrations		• Life often feels like a battle: a battle with our own struggles and sin (Rom. 7:21–25), with external influences and pressures. • Yet, Jesus' victory on the cross has defeated all the powers that bind and limit humanity: sin and death are defeated; Satan and his hosts are defeated. • Jesus' death on the cross was D-Day for God's people. In the famous day in World War II, the Allies overtook the beaches of Normandy and changed the course of the war. Jesus mortally wounded Satan and sealed his fate.

Metaphor	NATIONAL	Jesus allows us to become citizens of the kingdom of heaven.
Positive	CITIZEN	• Fellow citizens (Eph. 2:19) • Citizens of heaven (Phil. 3:20)
Negative	ALIEN	• Alien to a sinful world (1 Peter 2:11) • People looking for a country of their own (Heb. 11:13) • Longing for our real home (2 Peter 3:13)
Illustrations		• Being a citizen of a country provides identity, security, and rootedness. • Christians are citizens of God's kingdom. Our loyalties are to God and his will. • In a globalized world, where people move so fast and everywhere, the concept of citizenship takes new meanings. • Our identity, security and sense of community do not depend on the place or culture in which we were born. Rather, it depends on the values of the kingdom of God.

Citizenship in the Roman World

- The concept of Roman citizenship is the background for the Apostle Paul's use of citizenship as an illustration of salvation. The Apostle Paul was a Roman citizen by birth (Acts 22:25–29).

- Access to Roman citizenship was limited and difficult to obtain. Although many people achieved, earned, or were granted Roman citizenship, their citizenship was of a secondary kind. Even this secondary type of citizenship provided many rights and protections.

- These were some ways people could get Roman citizenship:
  ◇ Granted automatically to male children born from a Roman citizen.
  ◇ Freed slaves were granted a limited form of citizenship. In time, they could earn full citizenship. Their sons were full citizens.
  ◇ Soldiers who served for 25 years or more in the Roman legions were granted full citizenship. Their sons were also granted citizenship.
  ◇ Individuals who performed extraordinary services to the Roman Empire were also granted full citizenship.
  ◇ Individuals could buy citizenship at a very high price.

- When Christ frees us from slavery, he grants us full citizenship in the kingdom of God.

- In the Roman Empire, when slaves were freed, they became citizens.

Metaphor	TRUTH	Jesus offers the only truth that can lead us to God (John 14:6).
Positive	CORRECT/ TRUE	• Salvation as knowledge of the truth (1 Tim. 2:4) • The gospel is the word of truth (Eph. 1:13; John 17:17). • The truth of the gospel makes us free (John 8:32). • The Holy Spirit leads us to the truth (John 16:13).
Negative	ERROR/ FALSE	• False prophets deceive and lead astray (Ezek. 13:1–23; Matt. 24:11, 24). • False teachings lead to destruction (2 Peter 2:1–2).
Illustrations		• Traveling without a map can lead to an exciting adventure or a disastrous end. A map is helpful when we follow its instructions. A correct map will lead us faithfully. An incorrect map will lead us astray. • The words of the gospel lead us correctly to our final destination.

Metaphor	VISION	Jesus promises to open our eyes so we can see him and God's wonders (Isa. 42:7).
Positive	SIGHT	• Jesus opened the eyes of his disciples (Luke 24:31). • Jesus came to give sight (Luke 4:18–19; John 9:39).
Negative	BLINDNESS	• Sin is blindness (John 9:39–41). • Blind guides lead others astray (Matt. 23:16–17). • People blinded to the gospel (2 Cor. 4:4).
Illustrations		• In the Bible, physical blindness was a metaphor for spiritual blindness. • Jesus used this metaphor to teach about the gospel (see, John 9) • In the ancient world, only the "gods" were able to heal blindness. • Jesus restores both physical and spiritual sight to people. • Spiritual blindness has different causes: fear, unbelief, pride, greed, hatred, and egocentrism. Spiritual blindness prevents us from seeing God's doings in the world.

Blindness Healed by Jesus

- Jesus heals two blind men (Matt. 9:27–31)
- Jesus heals a man with demonic blindness (Matt. 12:22)
- Jesus restores sight to two men outside Jericho—one of whom was named Bartimaeus (Mark 10:46–52; Luke 18:35–43)
- Jesus heals a blind man at Bethsaida (Mark 8:22–26)
- Jesus gives sight to a man born blind (John 9:1–41)
- Jesus heals many people with blindness (Matt. 11:5; 21:14)

Metaphor	NAVIGATION	Jesus came to seek and save the lost. He promises to guide us to the right destination (Luke 19:10).	
Positive	FOUND	• The lost have been returned (1 Peter 2:25). • The Good Shepherd seeks the lost sheep (Matt. 18:12). • Jesus came to save what was lost (Luke 19:10). • Joy in heaven for the found (Luke 15:1–7) • Joy over the lost who is found (Luke 15:11–32)	
Negative	LOST	• We were lost (Isa. 53:6; Jer. 50:6; Mark 6:34).	
Illustrations		• The sense of being lost, especially in a hostile environment, produces many and strong emotions: fear, anxiety, anger, and disappointment. • The final problem is that lost people are incapable of reaching their destination. • Jesus reorients us toward our correct destination: God's kingdom. When Jesus saves us, we begin to walk in the direction that will lead us to our final destination in God's presence.	

Metaphor	AMBULATORY— RELATED TO WALKING	Jesus promises to walk alongside us: "And surely I am with you always, to the very end of the age" (Matt. 28:20).	
Positive	STANDING/ WALKING	• Walking on the path of righteousness (Prov. 8:20; 12:28) • The path of life revealed (Acts 2:28; Ps. 16:11) • Jesus keeps us from falling (Jude 1:24).	
Negative	FALLING/ STUMBLING	• Those burdened by sin stagger and fall (Isa. 3:8). • Those who do not know Christ will stumble over him (Rom. 9:32, 33; Isa. 8:14). • Unbelief on Jesus causes us to fall (1 Peter 2:8; Luke 20:18).	
Illustrations		• Walking in God's paths is a common metaphor in the Bible. • *Walking* brings to mind the idea of movement and journey, the satisfactions and benefits of traveling as well as the difficulties involved in it. • As we walk, we learn, grow, and move forward. • However, walking requires a direction, lest it becomes a mere wandering. • One way to understand sin is that one misses the mark, or one's destination. • Jesus gives us a new orientation. • The Holy Spirit is our compass, and the Scriptures our map. • Only by walking alongside Jesus can we reach God, our true destination.	

Metaphor	**PURITY**	Jesus promises to cleanse us completely from our sins (Heb. 9:14).
Positive	**PURE/CLEAN**	• Jesus purifies his people (Titus 2:14). • Jesus' blood purifies us from sin (1 John 1:9).
Negative	**IMPURITY/ DIRTY**	• Jesus did not call us to be impure (1 Thess. 4:7). • We were slaves to impurity (Rom. 6:19).
Illustrations		• Cleanliness and dirtiness are daily experiences in life. The idea of cleaning something to make it acceptable is easy to visualize. We clean our homes, our clothing, our bodies to make them presentable and pleasant for others. • Sin corrupts and makes people impure. • People cannot make themselves clean of this pollution on their own. However, God cleans us with Jesus' blood to make us acceptable, pleasant to himself.

Sin

- Disobeying God's law in deed or attitude is a common definition of sin. The Bible uses illustrations to explain the meaning of sin.
- One of these illustrations is the idea of missing the mark. The most common words for sin in the Old and the New Testaments have the basic meaning of someone missing the mark. When people disobey, rebel, or act on their iniquity, their actions and thoughts miss the mark of God's Law. Acting or thinking in a way that contradicts God's Law leads us in a path away from God.

Metaphor	**KNOWLEDGE**	Jesus gives us the knowledge of God to be saved, to grow and mature, and live a life that pleases God (1 Tim. 2:4; 2 Tim. 2:25).
Positive	**UNDERSTANDING**	• Jesus gives the knowledge of salvation (Luke 1:77). • The Spirit gives understanding of what Christ has done (1 Cor. 2:12). • We have wisdom from God (Eph. 1:8, 17; Col. 2:2–3; James 1:5).
Negative	**IGNORANCE**	• Lack of knowledge causes destruction (Hos. 4:6). • Life apart from God is a life of ignorance (1 Peter 1:14). • Foolishness separates us from God (Jer. 5:21; 10:8; Titus 3:3).
Illustrations		• The knowledge the Bible refers here is not only mental knowledge. It also means intimate knowledge. It is a knowledge that affects the mind and the heart. • To truly get to know a person, reading a biography, hearing from other people, or spending a few minutes with a person is not enough. One needs time and energy to develop a relationship. After that time, one *knows* the other person. • It is not only book knowledge that allows us to know God and obtain salvation; we need deep, relational knowledge of Jesus. • The Holy Spirit gives us this knowledge primarily through the Scriptures, prayer, and fellowship with other believers.

Metaphor	LIGHT	Jesus is the light that shines on our path toward God (John 12:46).
Positive	LIGHT	• Jesus is the light of the world (John 8:12). • Jesus' light shines in our hearts (2 Cor. 4:4–6). • Children of light (Eph. 5:8). • Jesus has rescued us from darkness (Col. 1:13). • Putting aside the deeds of darkness (Rom. 13:12).
Negative	DARK	• People living in darkness have seen a great light (Matt. 4:16). • Humans have loved darkness (John 3:19).
Illustrations		• A campfire in the wilderness provides light, warmth, safety, and sustenance. • The light helps campers to find their way back to the camp. It provides warmth for the night. It keeps wild animals away. It cooks food and purifies water. • In a similar way, Jesus provides us with guiding light, warmth, safety, and sustenance for our journey of life.

Darkness

For the biblical peoples and their surroundings, darkness had a special role in their imaginations.
• Darkness was directly connected to chaos (Gen. 1:2).
• Darkness was the sphere of the wicked (Prov. 2:13).
• Darkness was related to death (1 Sam. 2:9; Ps. 143:3).
• Darkness was a form of judgment (Isa. 5:30; 8:22; 47:5).
• Darkness is under God's control (Gen. 1:3–5; 2 Sam. 22:29)

Metaphor	FREEDOM	Jesus has promised us to make us free from all bondage (John 8:36).
Positive	DELIVERANCE	To free us to: • New life (Rom. 6:4) • Freedom to serve (Gal. 5:1, 13) • Eternal life (John 10:28)
Negative	SLAVERY	To free us from: • Sin (Rom. 6:18) • The curse of the law (Gal. 4:3–5) • The fear of death (Heb. 2:14–15)
Illustrations		• Many things bind us: self-interest, addictions, broken relationships, anger and bitterness, destructive pasts, and debts. Sin captures our minds and hearts. Only a miracle can break those bonds. • Jesus breaks these bonds and gives us new life. This new life gives us the freedom to serve God, to become the people God wants us to be.

Metaphor	AGRICULTURAL	By being connected to Jesus, God's people have new life, can be fruitful, and have an abundant life.
Positive	CONNECTION	• God is portrayed as a caring gardener (Isa. 5:1–7). • Jesus allows us to be saved by grafting us into the tree to become part of his people (Rom. 11:24). • God's people are like trees planted by streams of water (Ps. 1:3). • Only by being connected to Jesus, the true vine, can we bear fruit (John 1–8).
Negative	SEPARATION	• By pruning Israel, God allowed Gentiles to become part of God's people (Rom. 11:17–21). • People without Jesus are like chaff that the wind blows away (Ps. 1:4). • No one can bear fruit apart from Jesus (John 15:4, 5–6).
Illustrations		• Gardening has become a more common urban activity—and continues to be vital in rural communities. Grafting and pruning are common activities in gardening. • Gardeners, professional and amateur, understand how important pruning is for the care and productivity of plants. • Like a gardener caring for his plants, God cares for his people. • God takes each of us, lifeless chaff, and grafts us into the tree of his people to give us new life. • Being saved is like being a plant, which is cared for and fruitful, in God's garden.

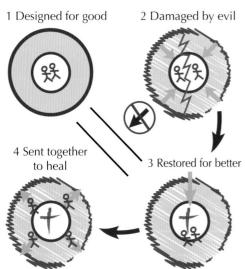

1 Designed for good

2 Damaged by evil

4 Sent together to heal

3 Restored for better

James Choung's Four Circles illustration shows God's original intention for his creation. God made humans to be and do good. However, sin affected our ability to do good. We became self-centered and enslaved to sin. Our sin breaks our relationship with God, nature, and one another.

Jesus came to restore humanity. His death on the cross liberated us from the slavery of sin and death.

Being free from sin, believers can become ambassadors of God. God is sending believers to heal relationships by preaching the good news of Jesus to a lost humanity.

Humans cannot move from circle 2 to 4 because sin has opened a gap that separates God from humans. Only through Christ is it possible to reach God.

Metaphor	CREATION	Jesus gives us the opportunity to be born again, to be a new creation. It is more than a fresh start. It is the right start (John 3:16–18).
Positive	NEW CREATION	• Jesus used the language of being born again (John 3:3, 7; 1 Peter 1:23). • Those born of God are children of God (1 John 3:9–10). • Christians are a new creation (2 Cor. 5:17; Gal. 6:15). • Jesus is presented as the second Adam (Rom. 5:15–17). • Jesus is the firstborn of the new creation (1 Cor. 15:27; 2 Cor. 5:17; Col. 1:15; Phil. 3:21).
Negative	OLD CREATION	• Sin transformed all of creation (Gen. 3:18; Rom. 8:22). • Sin entered through Adam's disobedience (Rom. 5:12–14). • This creation will pass and God will make all things new (Rev. 21:1; 2 Peter 3:13). • Nothing of the old creation can enter the kingdom of God (John 3:5).
Illustrations		• Jesus illustrated this point with a common object of his time: an unshrunk cloth to patch an old garment (Matt. 9:16). • The illustration is clear: when the garment is washed, the patch will shrink and tear the garment beyond repair. The old and the new do not mix with each other. • In the same way, God's grace requires a new heart (Ezek. 36:26). • Just as God makes us a new creation, God will make all things new one day (Rev. 21:1).

Creation to New Creation

Human Nature	What	When	Where	Who
Innocent	Good heart (Gen. 1:31)	In the beginning (past time)	In Eden (in paradise)	In Adam (our first parent)
Fallen	Corrupt heart (Gen. 3:19; 6:5,11,12; Rom. 3:9–19)	Upon the first sin (present time)	Upon the Earth (a wilderness outside Eden)	Upon all humanity
Redeemed	Transformed heart (Rom. 12:1–2)	At Christ's death and resurrection (present time)	At Calvary (outside the city of Jerusalem)	At conversion (all who are in Christ)
Perfect	Pure heart (Matt. 5:8; Heb. 12:14)	The age to come (future time)	The new heavens and earth (in the New Jerusalem)	God's people (believers in Christ, the last Adam)

Evangelism Plans

These four evangelism plans are ways to illustrate the gospel so its message is easier to understand. These four plans have helped millions of Christians around the world to bring the message of the gospel in a simple yet effective way.

Four Spiritual Laws (Campus Crusade for Christ)	➤ God loves you and offers a wonderful plan for your life (John 3:16; 10:10). ➤ Humans are sinful and separated from God. Thus, they cannot know and experience God's love and plan for their lives (Rom. 3:23; 6:23). ➤ Jesus Christ is God's only provision for humanity's sin. Through Jesus, you can know and experience God's love and plan for your life (Rom. 5:8; John 14:6). ➤ We must individually receive Jesus Christ as Savior and Lord; then we can know and experience God's love and plan for our lives (John 1:12; Eph. 2:8–9).
Bridge to Life (Navigators)	➤ The Bible teaches that God loves all humans and wants them to know him (John 10:10; Rom. 5:1). ➤ But humans have sinned against God and are separated from God and his love. This separation leads only to death and judgment (Rom. 3:23; Isa. 59:2). ➤ But there is a solution: Jesus Christ died on the cross for our sins (the bridge between humanity and God) (1 Peter 3:18; 1 Tim. 2:5; Rom. 5:8). ➤ Only those who personally receive Jesus Christ into their lives, trusting him to forgive their sins, can cross this bridge. Everyone must decide individually whether to receive Christ (John 3:16; John 5:24).
Steps to Peace with God (Billy Graham Crusade)	➤ Step 1. God's Plan ⇒ Peace and Life (Rom. 5:1; John 3:16; 10:10) ➤ Step 2. Humanity's Problem ⇒ Separation (Rom. 3:23; 6:23; Isa. 59:2) ➤ Step 3. God's Remedy ⇒ The Cross (1 Tim. 2:5; 1 Peter 3:18; Rom. 5:8) ➤ Step 4. Human Response ⇒ Receive Christ (John 1:12; 5:24; Rom. 10:9)
The Romans Road of Salvation	➤ Human Need (Rom 3:23) ➤ Sin's Penalty (Rom 6:23) ➤ God's Provision (Rom 5:8) ➤ The Person's Response (Rom 10:9)

Authors: William Brent Ashby, BT; Benjamin Galan, MTS, ThM, Adjunct Professor of OT Hebrew and Literature at Fuller Seminary.

Strong
in the Storm.

Lessons from Persecuted Christians
Stories of Modern-Day Disciples
The Four Stages of Persecution
How You Can Help Persecuted Christians

THERE IS SOMETHING about hardship that allows us to know God deeply. When times get really tough, we discover more about who God is and how he works. Christians who have endured persecution for their faith know this well.

There are no easy answers for why God allows his followers to face suffering. However, the lives of persecuted Christians reveal that even when things look out of control, believers can rest secure knowing that God is still in control. He is able to give courage, peace, and even joy to enable believers to stand strong in the storm. It is through these storms that believers discover God's love in new and powerful ways. The stories of persecuted Christians have much to teach us all.

Who are "persecuted Christians?"

Persecuted Christians are believers who face severe hardship, torture, imprisonment, or death because of their faith in Christ. They come from every age, race, and gender in more than 50 countries. Some believers remain steadfast, even to the point of death. Others give in to the pressure when faced with intimidation and impossible choices (such as to denounce Christ or see their children taken away). Persecuted Christians are as faithful, flawed, and human as any other Christian.

How are Christians persecuted?

- *Christians face severe hostility.* Intimidated by propaganda about Christianity, some Christians are forced to worship in secret and practice other religions in school or at work.

- *Christians are deprived of justice.* They are denied standard education, barred from all but menial labor, and told by crooked authorities to pay impossible fines. They are required to pay for baseless legal charges upheld by corrupt court systems. Those who must identify their faith on public documents can face discrimination. Christians are denied permits to build churches, which is the only way they can legally meet in groups.

- *Christians are imprisoned, tortured, and murdered.* They are harassed, attacked by mobs, beaten, kidnapped, interrogated about church locations and leaders, hunted by family or law enforcement, and publicly mocked.

Where are Christians persecuted?

Christians are persecuted in many countries around the world. Countries with totalitarian regimes (such as North Korea) or large populations of Muslims (such as Saudi Arabia) typically persecute Christians most severely. However, countries such as India, Vietnam, and Eritrea also have dismal records of abusing the religious freedom of Christians.

"Blessed are those who are persecuted for righteousness' sake, for theirs is the kingdom of heaven. Blessed are you when others revile you and persecute you and utter all kinds of evil against you falsely on my account. Rejoice and be glad, for your reward is great in heaven, for so they persecuted the prophets who were before you."

—Matthew 5:10–12

Six Lessons from Persecuted Christians

1 Sometimes you need to build yourself a cell.

WANG MINGDAO was one of the most well-known church leaders in China. He was an evangelist and an accomplished author. During the Chinese Cultural Revolution in the 1960s and 70s nearly all religious activity was severely persecuted. Wang Mingdao spent much of that time in solitary confinement in prison for his faith. He was finally released after 23 years of incarceration.

His years in prison have inspired millions of Chinese Christians. In the words of one Shanghai pastor, "Wang Mingdao proved that God existed—no one goes to jail for that long and comes out with their faith still intact if God is not real." This is Wang Mingdao's reflection on his experience:

When I was put in jail, I was devastated. I was sixty years old, at the peak of my powers. I was a well-known evangelist and wished to hold crusades all over China. I was an author. I wanted to write more books. I was a preacher. I wanted to study my Bible and write more sermons. But instead of serving God in all these ways, I found myself sitting alone in a dark cell. I could not use the time to write more books. They deprived me of pen and paper. I could not study my Bible and produce more sermons. They had taken it away. I had no one even to witness to, as the jailer for years just pushed my meals through a hatch. Everything that had given me meaning as a Christian worker had been taken away from me. And I had nothing to do. Nothing to do except get to know God. And for twenty years that was the greatest relationship I have ever known. But the cell was the means.

His advice to believers is this: *I was pushed into a cell, but you will have to push yourself into one. You have no time to know God. You need to build yourself a cell so you can do for yourself what persecution did for me—simplify your life and know God.[1]*

The busyness of life can quickly pile up unnoticed. It crowds out God before we even realize it. With never-ending "to do" lists, we must slow down and remind ourselves that the most important thing is knowing God. Even Christian service can become a distraction that keeps us from focusing on the greatest relationship we can know—our relationship with the Lord.

God keeps secrets.

NORTH KOREA is the most Communist society in the world and also the most religious. The new gods are [leaders] Kim Il Sung and his son, Kim Jong Il. They are believed to have supernatural powers, and the whole society is a vast coercive network to force continual worship of these "deities." The worship is not subtle. You can see bands of school children laying offerings at the feet of huge golden statues of these figures at the center of every town. Everyone is taught to revere them. Refuse and the penalty is to rot in a carbon copy camp of Auschwitz.[2]

R. J. Thomas was a missionary to China in the middle of the nineteenth century. He had a heart for Korea, but Korea was a hermit kingdom. No foreigners were allowed in. So Thomas went to China instead and bided his time. In 1865 the opportunity he had been waiting a lifetime for came along.

> An American ship, the SS General Sherman, was going to steam up the Taedong River to the capital, Pyong Yang, in hopes of luring the Koreans into trade. Thomas bought a berth on the ship, hoping to meet some scholars in Pyong Yang who spoke Chinese, and took as many Chinese Scriptures with him as he could carry on board.

> The trip was ill-fated. In a port on the way to the capital, some of the General Sherman's crew killed three Korean men in a barroom brawl. When they reached Pyong Yang, the rumors had grown to such an extent that it was impossible to berth. The people of Pyong Yang were convinced the foreigners had come for their children to make soup from their eyeballs. There was nothing to do but to turn around and head down the river.

> But they got stuck on a sandbank. Seeing them stranded the Korean defense lashed a series of small ships together, set them on fire, and they drifted to surround the General Sherman, which then caught fire. Everyone on board had to leap into the river. As they waded to shore, they were killed by the waiting Koreans.

Thomas also waded to shore. Before he could speak, a club swung with murderous force dashed his brains into the water, but his killer noticed he had not emerged with a cutlass, but was brandishing books. He picked up a couple of the sodden books. Drying them off, he separated the leaves and saw that they were nicely printed. He could not read but decided to paper the outside of his house with the pages, as was the custom at the time. Imagine his astonishment when he returned from the fields a few weeks later to find a clutch of scholars earnestly reading his walls. One of these scholars became a Christian by reading a Gospel portion plastered onto the wall. A generation later this scholar's nephew assisted in the first translation of the New Testament into Korean.

Yet Thomas never lived to see the fruit of his labor. He died, his life's purpose unfulfilled, his potential unrealized. For anyone aware of Thomas's death, his life was a mystery for years afterward. But his life was not in vain.[3]

Thomas's story shows us that it is OK to die unaware of one's life's meaning. Your life's purpose may remain a mystery to you, as may the events of your world, but that's OK. God is in control. We are relieved of the responsibility of understanding everything and the need to change it. God takes the rejected things of the earth and builds his eternal kingdom from them. One day all of God's secrets of why things happen will be revealed.

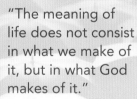

"The meaning of life does not consist in what we make of it, but in what God makes of it."
—Ronald Boyd-MacMillan

Weakness is a direct path to power.

COMING OUT of a Muslim extremist group in Egypt, Issa* was converted to Christ in his early twenties. He soon began to lead a church for Muslim converts—illegal in Egypt. The police arrested him and threw him in prison where he endured torture, whippings, and worst of all, confinement. He was crammed into a stone box no larger than five square feet. For one month he remained there, being fed every few days through a small slot in the door. While this kind of treatment caused many prisoners to go insane, he survived. In this deprived and weakened state, he found his most fulfilling moments with Christ. He shares his experience from despair to victory:

In great suffering you discover a different Jesus than you do in normal life. Normally we are able to hide from ourselves who we really are and what we are really like. The ego is well defended. But pain changes all that. Pain and suffering bring up to the surface all the weak points of your personality. You are too weak to mount the usual defenses and you just have to gaze at what you are really like.

I was a wreck in that cell. I was reduced to tears all the time. Crying, weeping, sobbing, and wailing in the never-changing utter darkness. I came face to face with how awful I really was. I saw all the horrible things I had done, all the horrible things I was. I kept seeing myself again and again in the crowd shouting, "Crucify him!"

But just as I was about to collapse into complete despair and self-loathing—and probably die—an incredible realization burst into the cell like an exploding star. It was this: Jesus loved me even right then, as I sat in my own filth, weak, helpless and broken, empty and sinful. Even in that state, He loved me, and Christ rushed in and filled me, and the filling was so great because I was so empty.[4]

Seeing clearly our failures and the wrongs we have done can be a devastating feeling. We think we have messed up our lives so much that God could not possibly want us anymore. But it is only then, when we come face to face with our broken and weak selves, that we begin to really understand how much God loves us. In our weakness we find power—not our own power, but the strength that comes from God's overwhelming love.

*Name changed to protect identity.

Overcoming is greater than deliverance.

STANDING FOR Jesus has a price. It can cost someone a good reputation, a job, education, family, friends, and even one's own life. The goal is to be willing to bear the price. That price is often collected in parts of China, where even today ordinary Christians continue to face martyrdom for following Christ. Such is the story of Brother Yuen. He was not a person of notoriety or position, just a quiet member of an underground church. Sister Chen, a witness to Brother Yuen's ordeal, explains how strength, rather than deliverance, was a powerful testimony to God.

Some years ago Brother Yuen was arrested. He was put into prison and then brought to the town square to be questioned openly. All believers were asked to join the accusation. The aim was to humiliate him and to scare others by killing him. I was one who was forced to join the chorus of accusations.

Brother Yuen stood in front of the government officials. No sad face, no frustration; just a peaceful face that smiled. It was as if I saw a life overflowing with peace and love. I saw Yuen very clearly. How in the world could he be so peaceful? I saw a light shine in his eyes that I had never seen there before. O yes, Brother Yuen had always been a faithful Christian. I remembered him as a quiet man, who lived with God without wanting to stand in the limelight. But now ... the light of life was shining from God's throne onto this imprisoned Christian.

Then he spoke, as he never had before: "I love Christ, I spread Christ, I trust in Christ, I follow Christ and I remain faithful to Christ. I am willing to accept what will come to me. I seek nothing else except Him. I hope that more people will come to accept Christ."

We came with sorrow, weakness and pain, yet we went back with comfort, strength and joy. We realized that this was not Brother Yuen, this was God, standing by, holding up, giving words to speak.[5]

Standing strong often requires believers not to overcome their circumstances, but instead to overcome their fear of those circumstances. It may be difficult to understand how in the midst of persecution, believers experience a sense of glory. However, the testimonies of persecuted Christians reveal that God is able to give them peace in a supernatural way. (See Acts 7:54–60 and Philippians 4:6–7.) We may pray for God to quickly deliver us from frightening or stressful situations, but sometimes God may instead choose to provide us with the courage and strength to endure within those circumstances.

5 Extreme hurt requires extreme forgiveness.

IN IRAN, 98% of the population is Muslim. Since the Islamic Revolution of 1979, the Iranian government has implemented Sharia Law, the fundamentalist Islamic law that covers aspects of everyday life and legal punishment. Under this system, leaving Islam and evangelizing among Muslims is strictly forbidden.

As a teenager in Iran, Takoosh had prayed that she might be allowed someday to marry a pastor, so that she could spend her life in the service of God. Her wish was fulfilled when she married Pastor Haik Hovsepian. But what lay ahead would not be easy.

Takoosh's husband held important positions as the general secretary of the Assemblies of God and the chairman of the Council of Protestant Ministers. On various occasions, he stated that he was willing to go to the utmost for his faith. Takoosh reflects: "Haik repeatedly said, 'We don't have to be afraid. We must trust in God.' But in my heart, I was afraid. Haik was full of love for people, even for his Muslim neighbors. They were welcome at the Church; they knew that he would help them in times of difficulty."

Then one day in 1994, Haik left to pick up a friend from the airport. He never returned. After twelve days, it became apparent that he had been killed at the behest of the Iranian government. According to the police, his body had been found in an alleyway in Teheran. He had been stabbed to death. Around that time, four other Iranian pastors were also murdered. They had refused to sign an official declaration that they would not evangelize among Muslims.

The day that Haik went missing is deeply engraved on the memory of Takoosh and her children.

Takoosh tells of her personal struggle: "I only had hatred in my heart, hatred for my enemies who had murdered Haik. I was not able to forgive them. I prayed with my lips, 'God, give me the strength to forgive,' but before I prayed, in my imagination I saw myself throwing mud at them. But one day a miracle happened. God taught me how I could forgive my enemies. I was asking for something which on the deepest level I did not want to ask for. But gradually, in a process of ups and downs which took months, God gave me the strength to pray more and more with my heart for those who had murdered my husband. God answered this prayer. Then I was no longer praying only with my lips, but from the depths of my heart. I had learned not only to trust in God and to lean on him, but also how you can forgive your enemies."[6]

GRACE DUBE'S husband was stabbed to death in South Africa. She tells of how her family found the ability to forgive in the midst of grief:

My husband was not alone when he was killed. One of my sons was with him, Benjamin Jr. He was only 12 years old and managed to escape. From behind a barrel he saw what they did to his father. He came running home to Soweto to tell me what had happened. Even though my husband had predicted what would happen I could not believe it had happened.

My son Benjamin went to his room and wept and wept, all night. Then the Lord did something in the heart of my boy. He heard a wonderful voice, like his father had heard. His father had often told him, "Benjamin, you must take my place to sing for the Lord if anything happens to me." Early the next morning I heard singing, coming from my son's bedroom. At first it was a broken voice, but then, it became clearer and clearer. I could hear my boy sing to the Lord. He sang a verse from the Scripture, "Father, forgive them, for they do not know what they are doing."

I could hardly control myself. O Lord, make me like my children. Help me to forgive. My son and I have sung this wonderful song together ever since, in many meetings, in many countries, to many people who are hurt—and who need to forgive also. Father, forgive us, because we too do not always know what we are doing.[7]

In Matthew 5:44, Jesus instructs believers to "Love your enemies and pray for those who persecute you." This may seem like an unrealistic task, something only for "super-Christians." But the testimonies from persecuted believers remind us that ordinary Christians really can find extraordinary love to forgive others just as Jesus forgave. The ability to forgive may not come immediately, but when we pray and ask the Lord for help, he will bring healing and love in ways we didn't know were possible.

We need reminders that our battles are ultimately spiritual, and so are our "enemies." Persecuted Christians can help us understand that those who do us wrong are not the real enemy; the enemy is the evil one who hates God.

"Your enemy the devil prowls around like a roaring lion looking for someone to devour. Resist him, standing firm in the faith, because you know that your brothers throughout the world are undergoing the same kind of sufferings. And the God of all grace, who called you to his eternal glory in Christ, after you have suffered a little while, will himself restore you and make you strong, firm and steadfast."
—1 Peter 5:8–10

Prayer is the ultimate fellowship.

WHEN PERSECUTED Christians are asked what other believers can do for them, the most common answer is, "Please pray for me." For believers who are isolated, imprisoned, and presumably forgotten, that hope of fellowship through prayer is a lifeline.

Gerhard Hamm, a Russian Christian who spent many years in prisons and labor camps in Northern Siberia, tells about one incident when God's people prayed.

One day, I was arrested together with 30 other brothers in Moscow. We were taken to the police station and locked up in an ice-cold room. It was a few days before Christmas and we thought we would probably not be home by then. It was no use complaining, so one of the brothers said, "Let's pray." We all knelt down on the cold concrete floor and then there followed a miraculous hour of prayer. The policeman was dumbfounded, but afterwards he said, "What kind of fanatics are you? How dare you pray in an atheist police station?" A long conversation followed.

Later on, an officer appeared and he said, "We don't know what to do with you. If we imprison one of you, he will convert another prisoner. If we imprison two, another two will be converted. Go home, you won't bother us there."

In the Bible, Daniel prayed in spite of the king's decree. He was aware that praying was dangerous, but he also realized that prayer was of vital importance. How odd that praying could cost him his life, while not praying would kill him spiritually. It was no difficult choice. To him, his relationship with God was more important than his position or his life. Prayer gives strength and opens doors. If it doesn't open doors of prison cells, it opens the hearts of people inside prisons. What a powerful weapon! Use it.[8]

"Were it lawful, I could pray for greater trouble for greater comfort sake."
—John Bunyan (1628–1688), written from jail

Prayer is where we fellowship with God and we are in harmonious companionship with believers. It is living "prayerfully" that brings survivors of great affliction to understand that prayer is where they discover the beauty and splendor of God. During prayer times, God's mercy, grace, and supernatural power are revealed in amazing ways. Prayer is vitally important! That's why the Bible tells us, "Never stop praying. Be thankful in all circumstances, for this is God's will for you who belong to Christ Jesus" (1 Thessalonians 5:17–18 NLT).

Four Stages of Persecution

STAGE 1:	Opposition
"Consider [Jesus] who endured such opposition from sinful men, so that you will not grow weary and lose heart." —Hebrews 12:3	Jesus repeatedly warned his followers that if the world hated him, it would hate them also (Luke 6:22). Intimidation and verbal opposition characterize the first stage of persecution. Unchecked ridicule of Christian institutions and principles is a strategic weapon in silencing the gospel. Attacking those beliefs through the media, politics, entertainment, publications, and schools ushers in the next phase where it is acceptable to attack the believer.

STAGE 2:	Personal Slander
"Blessed are you when people … falsely say all kinds of evil against you because of me." —Matthew 5:11	Christians may be robbed of their good reputation and their right to answer accusations against them. Insinuations or lies (often spread by way of the media) destroy reputations or cast doubt on an upstanding person. For example, a pastor in central Asia was shown on TV and, without reference to any evidence, labeled "an enemy of the state." His family members' pictures were also shown at the same time, causing them to be despised by their community.

STAGE 3:	Injustice (Discrimination)
"In his humiliation [Jesus] was deprived of justice." —Acts 8:33a	This stage relegates Christians to second-class citizenship with inferior legal, social, political, and economic status. Examples abound: ID cards in a country where Christianity is an unacceptable entry in the religion column; daughters abducted and their fathers unable to receive justice from the courts because they are Christians; expulsion from the community because one claims to be "born again."

STAGE 4:	Mistreatment
"Remember those in prison as if you were their fellow prisoners, and those who are mistreated as if you yourselves were suffering." —Hebrews 13:3	This stage includes the "big three:" torture, imprisonment and martyrdom. Persecution can arise from the state, the police or military, extremist organizations, militias, representatives of other religious groups, or even one's own family members. In many parts of the world, the attackers blame the victims by accusing the victims of committing violence and criminal activity. For example, in Eritrea, a small country in east Africa, the government has imprisoned hundreds of Christians—many kept in metal shipping containers.

How can I help persecuted Christians?

Get informed. Learn what is happening to the worldwide family of God through news and frontline organizations.

Pray. Respond with the first thing persecuted Christians request—your prayers.

- "Prayer isn't preparation for the battle; it is the battle."—*Brother Andrew, author of God's Smuggler and founder of Open Doors*

Get God's Word to them.
As one pastor in prison, nearly crippled for not relinquishing his Bible, said, "The Bible is life!"

- "I could go to prison for having this book, but this book can also set men free."—*Russian Christian after receiving a Bible*

- "The more I read, the more I want to read."—*Russian Christian after receiving his first Bible*

- "I wish I knew what was on the next page."—*Siberian Christian who had only one page of the Bible*

Participate in advocacy campaigns for religious freedom. Everyone should be free to choose Christ.

Tell their stories. Mostly, they feel they are a forgotten and broken segment of the church, when in reality they are the church triumphant, demonstrating faith and sacrifice as shown in the life of Jesus Christ.

Visit them. Go to them in prison or in their homes or churches.

Get involved. Volunteer with organizations and churches that work directly and confidentially to protect and strengthen persecuted believers. Some organizations include:

- Open Doors with Brother Andrew
  www.OpenDoorsUSA.org

- Barnabas Fund
  www.barnabasfund.org

- Christian Freedom International
  www.christianfreedom.org

- International Christian Concern
  www.persecution.org

- International Day of Prayer for the Persecuted Church
  www.persecutedchurch.org (Coalition of several ministries that remember persecuted Christians in prayer the second Sunday in November)

- Jubilee Campaign
  www.jubileecampaign.org

- Secret Believers
  www.secretbelievers.org

- Voice of the Martyrs
  www.persecution.com

Provide resources. Persecuted Christians need your financial assistance through organizations that deliver Bibles, church materials, spiritual leadership training, and legal counsel.

100 million
The number of Christians living in areas where they face persecution

400 million
The number of Christians living under the threat of persecution

Where are the worst places for Christians to live?

The World Watch List (at www.OpenDoorsUSA.org) ranks the countries where persecution of Christians is most severe. For the past two decades, North Korea, Saudi Arabia, and Iran have topped the list.[9]

- **North Korea** allows only the worship of "the beloved leader" Kim Jong Il and his father Kim Il Sung. Christians are seen as a threat, so increasing numbers of Christians have been sentenced to torture and starvation in labor camps or secretly executed. North Korea's border with China is virtually closed. Chinese authorities vigilantly pursue North Korean defectors and return them to North Korea to face a painful, prolonged death in labor camps.

- **In Saudi Arabia**, public non-Muslim worship is forbidden. Although Christians are generally allowed to worship in private, some have been arrested, issued with death threats, and forced into hiding. Most Saudi believers must keep their faith secret or else risk being killed by family members in honor killings.

- **In Iran**, the police closely watch and crack down on house churches. Muslims found guilty of converting to Christianity could face a death sentence. Church services may be monitored by the secret police. Believers are often discriminated against, making it difficult to find and keep jobs.

6.40% The annual growth of Islam

1.46% The annual growth of Christianity

Terms & Definitions

Christian Martyr A believer who is killed for following Jesus Christ.

Cultural Revolution in China A time of social upheaval lasting approximately from 1966 to 1976, led by Mao Zedong, the leader of the Communist Party, to solidify socialism in China. During this time religious activity was severely persecuted and many religious buildings were burned or looted.

Honor killing A killing of a family or tribe member (often a woman or teenage girl) by the family or tribe because they believe the member has dishonored the entire group. The killing is believed to absolve the family of the dishonor and restore their standing within the group.

House church or underground church A church where believers must meet in secret because they are not allowed building permits for churches, or because meeting openly could bring about persecution of the congregation and its resources.

Islamic Revolution in Iran The 1979 overthrow of Iran's monarchy which was replaced by an Islamic Republic said to be a government based upon Sharia Law.

Mahdi The Islamic Messiah that is prophesied to come in the future near the world's end by Sunnis, while Shi'ites believe he has been here and is now in hiding.

Religious Persecution The deliberate act of a government, culture, family, or individual to restrict or punish a person or group based on faith.

Sharia Law The fundamental Islamic Law that covers many aspects of everyday life and legal punishment. Countries that enact Sharia Law severely punish conversions from Islam, at times, to the point of death. Such countries include Saudi Arabia, Kuwait, Bahrain, Yemen, and United Arab Emirates.

Shi'a The second largest denomination of Islam which believes in the traditions of Shi'a. Thought to be 10–15% of all Muslims.

Sunni The largest branch of Islam, which believes in the traditions of the Sunna. Generally considered to be 85–90% of all Muslims.

Notes

1 Ronald Boyd-MacMillan, *Faith that Endures* (Fleming H. Revell), ©2006 Open Doors International, 307–308. Used by permission.

2 Ibid., 312. Used by permission.

3 Ibid., 313–314. Used by permission.

4 Ibid., 319–320. Used by permission.

5 Jan Pit, *Day by Day with the Persecuted Church* (Sovereign World, Ltd), ©1995 Open Doors International, 353. Used by permission.

6 Open Doors Holland, *12 Discoveries by the Persecuted Church* ©2009 Open Doors Holland. Used by permission.

7 Jan Pit, *Day by Day,* 201. Used by permission.

8 Ibid., 30. Used by permission.

9 Although some of the worst offenders on the World Watch List provide laws and agree to United Nations resolutions supposedly ensuring religious freedom, minority religions rarely receive any meaningful protection.

Contributors: Writers and researchers of Open Doors USA and Open Doors International.
Photos provided by Open Doors unless otherwise specified.

Rose Bible Basics:

Being Jesus' Disciple

A FREE downloadable version of this guide is available at rose-publishing.com. Click on "News & Info," then on "Downloads."

The **leader guide** covers each chapter of this book and includes teaching tips and additional resources.

The **study guide** includes reproducible worksheets and discussion questions for each chapter.

What participants will gain from this study:
- Understand their identity in Christ.
- Learn how to know and accept God's will for their lives.
- Gain practical guidance in spiritual disciplines.
- Know how to discern the truth and steer clear of false teachings.
- See what God's Word says about being faithful stewards.
- Learn 24 ways to explain the good news of Jesus.
- Read inspiring stories of modern-day disciples who stayed strong through persecution.

LEADER GUIDE

Spend time in prayer before each session and pray for each participant.

CHAPTER 1: WHO I AM IN CHRIST
Main Idea
As a believer in Christ, you are a child of God—loved, saved, and renewed.

Teaching Tips
Introduce participants to the purposes of this study. Ask them what they hope to gain from the study or why they joined this study.

As you teach this session, be sure to highlight why it is important for believers to understand their identity in Christ. Explain how it can make a difference in our daily lives, at our jobs, with our families, and for our future hope.

Digging Deeper
Following Jesus pamphlet (Rose Publishing, 2005). An easy-to-understand guide for new believers.

CHAPTER 2: KNOWING GOD'S WILL
Main Idea
God has a purpose for each of us. We can trust God to love us and work all things in our lives for good.

Teaching Tips
Lead by example. You can encourage participants to open up and share their stories by giving your own testimony. Remember to include specifics and concrete examples of how you have seen God's will in your life.

Make the *Four Things You Can Do* worksheet into something participants can do as a group. For example: create the cards or prayer journals together; organize a volunteer service; pick names out of a hat and ask each person pray for the individual whose name they chose every day until the next meeting. Pray that they would know and live in God's will daily.

Digging Deeper
Just Do Something: A Liberating Approach to Finding God's Will by Kevin DeYoung (Moody, 2009)

Plan B: What Do You Do When God Doesn't Show Up the Way You Thought He Would? by Pete Wilson (Thomas Nelson, 2010)

Bible Promises for Hope and Courage pamphlet (Rose Publishing, 2006)

CHAPTER 3: SPIRITUAL DISCIPLINES

Main Idea

Spiritual disciplines help us change our sinful habits into good habits that make us more like Christ.

Teaching Tips

Set aside some time during the session to practice several of the spiritual disciplines: Read a Scripture passage; spend time in silent reflection; pray together; worship together in song or liturgy. Ask participants to share with the group if God laid anything particular on their hearts during this time.

Be aware that as you discuss spiritual disciplines some participants may feel guilty or judge themselves as lesser Christians. Remember to emphasize that feelings of guilt or failure are not reasons to give up on the spiritual disciplines, but may be cues to set realistic goals or to learn how to rely on God rather than on our own strength of will or determination.

Digging Deeper

Celebration of Discipline: The Path to Spiritual Growth by Richard J. Foster (HarperOne, 1998)
How to Study the Bible pamphlet (Rose Publishing, 2007)
One-Year Bible Reading Plan pamphlet (Rose Publishing, 2009)
Metamorpha; an online community for Christian spiritual formation; www.metamorpha.com

CHAPTER 4: WHY TRUTH MATTERS

Main Idea

Discerning the truth from lies is essential to healthy, authentic Christian faith.

Teaching Tips

Before the session, familiarize yourself with the teachings of the religious and cult groups mentioned in this chapter. (See www.apologeticsindex.org and www.thecenters.org.)

If the discussion time becomes controversial or argumentative, use the disagreement as a teaching opportunity; allow for disagreement, not accusation. Remind participants that discernment is a process, and we shouldn't assume we have all the right answers up front. It's about relying on God to show us the truth as we research the claims of others, dig into God's Word, and pray for spiritual eyes to see the truth.

Digging Deeper

See "Recommended Reading" and "Discernment Ministries" at the end of the chapter.
Also see *Rose Bible Basics: Christianity, Cults & Religions* (Rose Publishing, 2008)

CHAPTERS 5: WHAT THE BIBLE SAYS ABOUT MONEY

Main Idea

God cares about our faithfulness with money—whether it is a lot or a little. We must always remember to keep God at the center of our finances.

Teaching Tips

Open the session by having participants brainstorm together: What kinds of messages do you hear about money from advertisements, family members, church leaders, coworkers, financial advisors, politicians, and others? Write all their answers on a whiteboard or easel pad. After the lesson time, go back to the list of messages and compare the list to what the Bible says about money.

At the end of the session have participants gather in a circle and place in the center their wallets, car keys, house keys, credit cards, and so forth. As a group, pray together affirming that everything we own has come from God and ultimately belongs to him. Pray for wisdom to know how to use all our resources for God's glory and his kingdom.

Digging Deeper

The Challenge of the Disciplined Life: Christian Reflections on Money, Sex & Power by Richard J. Foster (HarperSanFrancisco, 1985)

Money, Possessions, and Eternity revised edition by Randy Alcorn (Tyndale House, 2003)

CHAPTER 6: 24 WAYS TO EXPLAIN THE GOSPEL

Main Idea

It is important to explore, learn, appropriate, and use the illustrations the Bible itself uses to explain what Jesus accomplished on the cross.

Teaching Tips

Begin the session by giving each participant a blank piece of paper and pen. Ask participants to take a few minutes to write down in their own words what the gospel is. Then ask participants to voluntarily share what they wrote. Read 1 Corinthians 15:1–8 where the apostle Paul explains the gospel to the Corinthian believers.

Digging Deeper

The God Conversation: Using Stories and Illustrations to Explain Your Faith by J.P. Moreland, Tim Muelhoff, and Lee Strobel (InterVarsity, 2007)

Life of Jesus pamphlet (Rose Publishing, 2009). Answers to the questions of why Jesus came, what he taught, and why he died and rose again.

CHAPTER 7: STRONG IN THE STORM

Main Idea

We can learn valuable lessons about following Jesus from the stories of other disciples who have stood strong through tough times.

Teaching Tips

Approach this chapter from the angle of discipleship. The best way to know what discipleship looks like is to see it in action, lived out by other disciples who have followed Jesus even when it was extremely difficult.

Does your church participate in the International Day of Prayer for the Persecuted Church? If not, consider having your group take the lead or get involved in the next Day of Prayer. (See www.persecutedchurch.org for details.)

Be sure to set aside some time during the session to pray specifically for persecuted believers.

Digging Deeper

Faith that Endures: The Essential Guide to the Persecuted Church by Ronald Boyd-MacMillan (Revell, 2006)

Day by Day with the Persecuted Church: 365 Daily Readings by Jan Pit (Sovereign World, 1995)

Open Doors: Serving persecuted Christians worldwide, www.opendoorsusa.org

FEEDBACK

To improve future studies, be sure to get feedback from the group about teaching style, meeting location, discussion time, material covered, length of study, and group size. Choose a method that best suits your group: Anonymous evaluation sheet, e-mail response or questionnaire, open discussion. (See the feedback questions at the end of the study guide.)

The inclusion of a work or website does not necessarily mean endorsement of all its contents or of other works by the same author(s).

STUDY GUIDE

The study guide which begins on the following page includes a reproducible worksheet and discussion questions for group discussion or personal reflection.

Who I am in Christ

Worksheet

Choose 10 of the "I am's" from this chapter that are most meaningful to you. Then complete the sentence ("This means that I...") with something specific and personal to your own circumstances in life.

1. I am _____. This means that I am _____
   _____
   _____

2. I am _____. This means that I am _____
   _____
   _____

3. I am _____. This means that I am _____
   _____
   _____

4. I am _____. This means that I am _____
   _____
   _____

5. I am _____. This means that I am _____
   _____
   _____

6. I am _____. This means that I am _____
   _____
   _____

7. I am _____. This means that I am _____
   _____
   _____

8. I am _____. This means that I am _____
   _____
   _____

9. I am _____. This means that I am _____
   _____
   _____

10. I am _____. This means that I am _____
   _____

Who I am in Christ

Discussion Questions

1. What would you tell a new Christian who *believes* that he or she is new creation in Christ, but doesn't *feel* like he or she is?

2. What does it mean to be made in the image of God?

3. In your own words, how would you explain what it means to have a "new mind" (Rom. 12:1–2)?

4. Why can *only* Christ's blood shed on the cross allow us to have a new, wonderful identity?

5. How does understanding your identity in Christ help you become a better disciple of Jesus?

Knowing God's Will

Worksheet

Four Things You Can Do

- *Create daily reminders.* On 3x5 cards, write each of the headings in the section "What do I need to remember about God's leading?" (For example: write "#2. I won't miss God's plan if my heart is set on pleasing him.") Place the cards where you will see them easily and often (For example: On your desk, in your locker, on your mirror, your closet.)

- *Keep a prayer journal.* On the first day of each week write down your prayer requests and consistently pray about them. At the end of the month look back over your requests and see how God answered them. Was it a "yes" answer, a "no" answer, or "wait"? This will help you see how God is working in your life.

- *Start serving others.* Sometimes we need quiet time alone with God to listen to him, but remember that God also works in your life through your active service to others. Don't let uncertainty about God's will paralyze you from helping others. Find opportunities to volunteer in your church or community.

- *Ask someone to pray for you.* As a part of the body of believers, you are not alone! When you have a tough decision to make, find a friend, pastor, church leader, or a family member and ask him or her to pray for God to show you his will.

Discussion Questions

1. Why do you think that God sometimes has us wait for him, rather than just answering our prayers right away?

2. Read Romans 8:38–39. In your own words, how would you describe this kind of love?

3. What do you do when you pray about a decision you have to make, but don't have a clear "yes" or "no" from God?

4. If a friend told you that she felt like she has missed God's will for her life, what would you say to her?

5. Share with the group about a time when God changed a bad situation in your life into a good outcome. Looking back, what do you know now that you didn't know then about how God works?

Spiritual Disciplines

Worksheet

For each of the spiritual disciplines below, write one practical thing you can do to grow in them. Remember to keep it realistic and achievable. For example, it might mean getting to church service on time so you can participate fully in the worship through music time. Or it might mean reading a book or talking with your pastor to learn more about a spiritual discipline that you don't quite understand or don't know how to do.

1. **Bible Reading/Study** _____

    _____

2. **Prayer** _____

    _____

3. **Fasting** _____

    _____

4. **Worship** _____

    _____

5. **Service** _____

    _____

6. **Solitude** _____

    _____

7. **Discernment** _____

    _____

8. **Evangelism** _____

    _____

Discussion Questions

1. Which spiritual discipline do you practice most often? Which one the least?

2. Do any of the spiritual disciplines cause you concern or make you uncomfortable? Why do you think this is so?

3. What are the spiritual disciplines for? And what are they not for?

4. What are some of the purposes of the spiritual discipline of solitude?

5. If a believer does not practice the spiritual disciplines often enough, does this put his or her salvation in jeopardy? Why or why not?

Why Truth Matters

Worksheet

Look up each of the passages below. In your own words, write down what each passage teaches about discerning the truth.

John 14:16–17 & John 16:12–13

_____

_____

1 Corinthians 15:1–8

_____

_____

1 Corinthians 2:12–16

_____

_____

1 Thessalonians 5:19–22

_____

_____

2 Timothy 3:12–16

_____

_____

Discussion Questions

1. If a Christian friend were following a false teacher on TV, the radio, or through a book, how would you approach your friend?
2. What would you do if you were concerned that a leader in your church was teaching a false doctrine? How would you approach the situation?
3. What role does the church and other believers have in discernment?
4. How can we discern whether a vision or miracle is true or false? Can we always know?
5. How is discernment a part of being a disciple of Jesus?

What the Bible Says about Money

Worksheet

Take a look at the diagram below. Mark on the spectrum where you are at for each of the points. Don't over-think your responses or try to find the "right" answer; just respond honestly about your typical attitude toward each of these aspects of money.

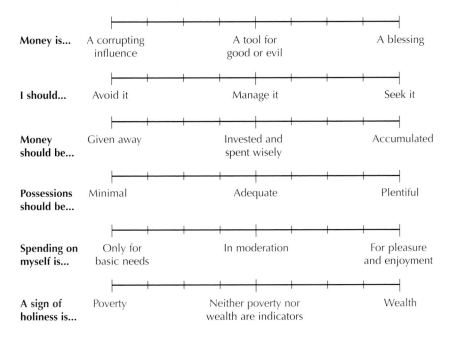

Money is...	A corrupting influence	A tool for good or evil	A blessing
I should...	Avoid it	Manage it	Seek it
Money should be...	Given away	Invested and spent wisely	Accumulated
Possessions should be...	Minimal	Adequate	Plentiful
Spending on myself is...	Only for basic needs	In moderation	For pleasure and enjoyment
A sign of holiness is...	Poverty	Neither poverty nor wealth are indicators	Wealth

After reading this chapter, how might you want your view of money to change on any of the aspects above?

Discussion Questions

1. What kinds of messages do you hear about money from advertisements, family members, church leaders, coworkers, financial advisors, politicians, and others? How do these compare to what the Bible says?

2. Why do you think there are so many verses in the Bible about money and wealth?

3. How does giving generously benefit not only the recipient, but also the giver?

4. What is the connection between money in our lives and being Jesus' disciple?

5. What are some practical things you can do—or avoid doing—to help you be content with what you have?

24 Ways to Explain the Gospel

Worksheet

The gospel is good news for all who believe. Using 20 of the illustrations in this chapter, create a list of what we were before coming to Christ and what we are now after accepting the gospel. (The first two are done for you.)

We were once:	We are now:
1. Dead	1. Alive
2. Immature	2. Mature
3.	3.
4.	4.
5.	5.
6.	6.
7.	7.
8.	8.
9.	9.
10.	10.
11.	11.
12.	12.
13.	13.
14.	14.
15.	15.
16.	16.
17.	17.
18.	18.
19.	19.
20.	20.

Discussion Questions

1. Which of the illustrations of salvation have you heard most often? Which ones least often?

2. See the four evangelism plans at the end of the chapter. Can you think of other evangelism plans you've heard or used to explain the gospel?

3. How do illustrations help us better understand what "salvation" means?

4. After reading this chapter, how do these biblical illustrations help you better understand what it means to be a disciple of Jesus?

Strong in the Storm

Worksheet

See "How Can I Help Persecuted Christians?" in this chapter. Write down four things you can do. Remember to make your goals specific and realistic.

1. _____

_____

2. _____

_____

3. _____

_____

4. _____

_____

Discussion Questions

1. Read John 15:19–21. Why is persecution an expected part of a believer's life?

2. What types of persecution do Christians in your culture or society face? (See "Four Stages of Persecution.")

3. What persecutions have you endured because of your faith?

4. Which of the six lessons was most meaningful to you? Why?

5. Look back over the chapters in this book. How can things like our identity in Christ, the spiritual disciplines, or discerning the truth prepare us to stand strong when faced with persecution?

Strong in the Storm

Write Your Own Story

You may not have faced persecution like the believers you read about, but everyone as a disciple of Jesus has been through hard times. Write down your experience and tell what you learned about God through it. Where did you see God's love through that storm in your life? Then share your story with a friend or your study group.

_____

_____

_____

_____

_____

_____

_____

_____

_____

_____

_____

_____

_____

_____

_____

_____

_____

_____

_____

FEEDBACK

1. What did you learn through this study that deepened your relationship with God and/or helped you understand biblical teachings better?

_____

_____

2. What was your favorite thing about this study, and why?

_____

_____

3. How could the meeting location, setting, length, or time be improved?

_____

_____

4. Did you think the material covered was too difficult, too easy, or just right?

_____

_____

5. What would you like to see different about the group discussions?

_____

_____

6. What would you like to see different about the activities?

_____

_____

7. What topic would you like to learn more about?

_____

_____

MORE Rose Bible REFERENCE
Bible Reference Made Easy

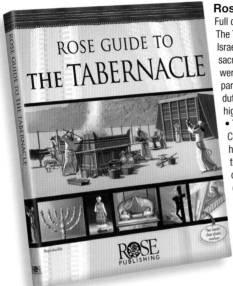

Rose Guide to the Tabernacle
Full color with clear overlays and reproducible pages
The Tabernacle ("tent of meeting") was the place where the Israelites worshiped God after the Exodus. Learn how the sacrifices, utensils, and even the structure of the tabernacle were designed to show us something about God. See the parallels between the Old Testament sacrifices and priests' duties, and Jesus' service as the perfect sacrifice and perfect high priest. See how:
• The Tabernacle was built • The sacrifices pointed Jesus Christ • The design of the tent revealed God's holiness and humanity's need for God • The Ark of the Covenant was at the center of worship. Clear plastic overlays show inside/outside of the tabernacle; plus dozens of reproducible charts. You may reproduce up to 300 copies of any chart free of charge for your classroom. 128 pages.

Finalist in the Christian Book Award

Deluxe "Then and Now" Bible Maps
Book with CD-ROM!
See where Bible places are today with "Then and Now" Bible maps with clear plastic overlays of modern cities and countries. This deluxe edition comes with a CD-ROM that gives you a JPG of each map to use in your own Bible material as well as PDFs of each map and overlay to create your own handouts or overhead transparencies. PowerPoint fans can create their own presentations with these digitized maps.

Hardcover. ISBN-13: 9781596361638

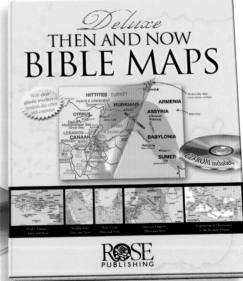

INCLUDES DISK

Other Rose Publishing Books

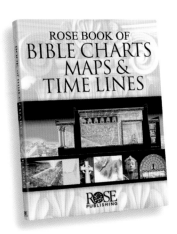

Rose Book of Bible Charts, Maps & Time Lines

Dozens of popular Rose Publishing Bible charts, maps, and time lines in one spiral-bound book. Reproduce up to 300 copies of any chart free of charge.

- Christianity, Cults & Religions
- Denominations Comparison
- Christian History Time Line
- How We Got the Bible
- Tabernacle
- Temple and High Priest
- Islam and Christianity

- Jesus' Genealogy
- Bible Time Line
- Bible Bookcase
- Bible Overview
- Ark of the Covenant
- Bible maps
- Trinity, and more.

192 pages. Hardcover.   ISBN-13: 9781596360228

Rose Book of Bible Charts 2

Here are dozens of popular Rose charts in one book! Topics include • Bible Translations comparison chart • Why Trust the Bible? • Heroes of the Old Testament • Women of the Bible • Life of Paul • Christ in the Old Testament • Christ in the Passover • Names of Jesus • Beatitudes • Lord's Prayer • Where to Find Favorite Bible Verses • Christianity and Eastern Religions • Worldviews Comparison • 10 Q & A on Mormonism/Jehovah's Witnesses/ Magic/Atheism and many others! Hardcover with a spine covering a spiral binding. 240 pages ISBN: 9781596362758

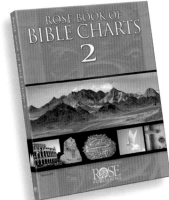

Rose Book of Bible & Christian History Time Lines

Six thousand years and 20 feet of time lines in one hard-bound cover! This unique resource allows you to easily store and reference two time lines in book form. These gorgeous time lines printed on heavy chart paper, can also be slipped out of their binding and posted in a hallway or large room for full effect.

• The 10-foot Bible Time Line compares Scriptural events with world history and Middle East history. Shows hundreds of facts; includes dates of kings, prophets, battles, and key events.

• The 10-foot Christian History Time Line begins with the life of Jesus and continues to the present day. Includes key people and events that all Christians should know. Emphasis on world missions, the expansion of Christianity, and Bible translation in other languages. These two time lines are connected end-to-end to form one long teaching aid. Hardcover. ISBN-13: 9781596360846

MORE Rose Bible Basics

Why Trust the Bible?
Is the Bible an ancient document that has been tampered with? Has it been edited many times over the centuries and now is filled with errors? How can we know what the Bible really said when the originals no longer exist? 128 pages ISBN: 9781596362017

Jesus
This easy-to-understand book provides a biblically centered approach to learning who Jesus is and why his powerful message of salvation matters today. 128 pages, ISBN: 9781596363243

Christianity, Cults & Religions
This book clarifies the differences between the beliefs and practices of various religions, cults, and new religious movements. Includes topics such as: Who is God? Who is Jesus Christ? What is salvation? What happens after death? 128 pages ISBN: 9781596362024

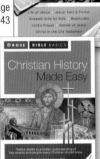

Christian History Made Easy
This easy-to-read book brings to life the most important events and people in Christian history that every believer should know. 224 pages, ISBN: 9781596363281

Names of God and Other Bible Studies
Contains favorite Bible studies to use in small groups, church groups, and for individual study. 128 pages ISBN: 9781596362031

God in Real Life
To navigate life's tough choices, teens and young adults need a real relationship with God in their real life. This book provides clear, biblical answers to their questions. 128 pages, ISBN: 9781596363250

Where to Find It in the Bible
Handy, full-color companion for Bible study and teaching. Helps you locate: • Your favorite Bible verses by topic • 100 prayers in the Bible • Important people of the Bible • 100 prophecies fulfilled by Jesus • 52 key Bible stories

128 pages ISBN: 9781596363441

The Bible at a Glance
Introduction to basic Bible knowledge. Contains a Bible overview of each book of the Bible, a Bible time line comparing Bible history and world history, steps to studying the Bible, Then & Now Bible maps, and more. 128 pages ISBN: 9781596362000

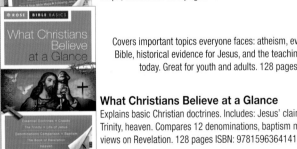

Myth-Busters
Covers important topics everyone faces: atheism, evolution, reliability of the Bible, historical evidence for Jesus, and the teachings of "spiritual" leaders today. Great for youth and adults. 128 pages ISBN: 9781596363458

What Christians Believe at a Glance
Explains basic Christian doctrines. Includes: Jesus' claims, creeds, the Trinity, heaven. Compares 12 denominations, baptism methods, and views on Revelation. 128 pages ISBN: 9781596364141

Free, downloadable study guide at rose-publishing.com.
Click on "News & Info," then on "Downloads."